ALAN MURIE

CW00493781

THE RIGHT TO BUY?

Selling Off Public and Social Housing

POLICY PRESS SHORTS POLICY & PRACTICE

First published in Great Britain in 2016 by

Policy Press
University of Bristol
1-9 Old Park Hill
Bristol
BS2 8BB
UK
+44 (0)117 954 5940
pp-info@bristol.ac.uk
www.policypress.co.uk

North America office:
Policy Press
c/o The University of Chicago Press
1427 East 60th Street
Chicago, IL 60637, USA
t: +1 773 702 7700
f: +1 773 702 9756
sales@press.uchicago.edu
www.press.uchicago.edu

British Library Cataloguing in Publication Data
A catalogue record for this book is available from the British Library.

Library of Congress Cataloging-in-Publication Data
A catalog record for this book has been requested.

ISBN 978 1 44733 207 7 (paperback)
ISBN 978 1 44733 209 1 (ePub)
ISBN 978 1 44733 210 7 (Mobi)

Cover design by Policy Press
Front cover: image kindly supplied by Getty
Printed and bound in Great Britain by CMP, Poole
Policy Press uses environmentally responsible print partners

Contents

List of tables and figures

Tables

Figures

About the author

Alan Murie is Emeritus Professor of Urban and Regional Studies at the University of Birmingham, UK.

Acknowledgements

My thanks go to Steve Forrest, Chris Watson, Gill Whitting and Peter Williams for comments made at various stages in writing this book.

1
INTRODUCTION

The year 2015 marked 35 years since the introduction of the Right to Buy – a flagship policy of Prime Minister Margaret Thatcher's government elected in 1979, and the most significant and lucrative act of privatisation associated with that or subsequent UK governments. The policy gave almost all tenants of public sector landlords the 'right to buy' their dwelling, and resulted in the sale of some 2 million dwellings in the UK between 1980 and 2015. In the same period, new additions to the stock of social rented housing fell far short of the volume of sales, and housing provided by local authorities and housing associations declined significantly.

The Right to Buy was always controversial, but media and other accounts focused on the successes – the stories of tenants who had bought their houses and the popularity of the policy. The government marketed the policy and periodically reinvented it to reassert its merits and to revive public interest. Reservations about the policy and its cumulative effects were more cautiously expressed, and for a long time arguments that the funds generated by selling houses should be reinvested in housing to ensure that future generations could obtain good quality, affordable housing were ignored.

There were no steps to reinvest capital receipts from council house sales in social housing before 1997 when concerns about value for money also began to inform policy modifications across the UK. Further changes followed to limit and then abolish the Right to Buy in

Scotland and Wales, but in England, after 2010, the policy was revived and relaunched with increased incentives to buy, and also after 2012, with commitments to replace sold council houses on a one-for-one basis. Proposals and agreements in 2015 and 2016 further extended the Right to Buy and divergence in approach between different parts of the UK.

Throughout 35 years of the Right to Buy, and the debates leading up to it, there have been different views of its impact and unanticipated consequences. In 2016, however, we are in a position to consider longstanding anxieties about the Right to Buy, its long-term impact, and the effects of its extension in England.

The Right to Buy was introduced in 1980 following a period of sustained progress in addressing key housing problems in the UK. Nineteenth-century policy-makers had been reluctant to intervene in the private property market, but a growing population, industrialisation and urbanisation generated increasing housing shortages, insecure, overcrowded and insanitary housing – and the private sector failed to respond adequately.

While the economy grew, housing conditions deteriorated. Local and national political debates increasingly focused on housing problems, and the ability to improve housing conditions became a test of government and the political system. Successive tentative policy interventions had limited impact but, after 1919, a series of experiments successfully established local authorities, supported by Exchequer subsidy, as major providers of good quality housing. The combination of a vigorous private sector housebuilding industry and sustained public sector housing procurement transformed the housing situation.

By 1939 there had been significant progress in addressing housing shortages, and this successful formula was reinvigorated after 1945. There was cross-party support for major investment in council housebuilding, supplemented by a new towns programme. By the 1970s investment in new public sector housing was operating alongside public policy support for home ownership through tax reliefs and other measures, including urban renewal. This mixed approach and the wider availability of building society loans for home ownership had increased housing supply, reduced unhealthy housing and facilitated slum clearance.

Throughout the growth of council housing between 1919 and 1979 there were differences of emphasis and detail, but there was broad consensus about how to improve housing across the UK. A large and successful council housing sector was a distinctive feature of British towns and cities, and played a critical role in shaping housing, the welfare state and the UK economy. Government policies supported expansion of both council housing and home ownership at the expense of private renting. Local housing authorities developed expertise and capacity in planning, building and managing housing and in supporting private sector housing improvement.

Local housing problems remained, and comprehensive local housing strategies used a range of policies and powers (related to land, planning, building, providing loans and grants, acquisition, managing and selling housing) for all tenures and all types of household, and working with other agencies. By the late 1970s one in three dwellings in the UK were owned by local authorities and new towns, and there was complacency because of the real inroads made into housing shortages and unhealthy housing. The main political parties, especially because of the costs of the public housing programme, had switched their attention from building more council housing to competing to promote home ownership. With the majority of people well housed, housing policy had fallen down the political agenda, and problems faced by the minority still in inadequate or inappropriate dwellings had reduced political importance.

The Right to Buy introduced by the Conservative government elected in 1979 broke the established pattern of support for both council housing and home ownership. Members of the new government regarded it as having been a vote winner. It was part of an approach variously regarded as providing neo-Conservative (supporting the family and promoting stability) or neoliberal (increasing reliance on markets) alternatives to collective welfare state provision. The ambition to promote locally distinctive policies for all tenures and all types of household gave way to a centrally driven, single-minded concern to expand individual home ownership and market processes. The policy involved the same approach everywhere, irrespective of local needs or politics, and the policy's success was assessed simply by the volume of sales it delivered, and the growth in home ownership that followed.

This new approach to housing policy involved an experiment, much as had the policies that established council housing 60 years previously. In 1979 exponents of housing privatisation asserted that state activity crowded out the market: reduced council activity would, therefore, stimulate private investment. The disciplines of the market would be more effective than those of public bureaucracies. If the Right to Buy had followed other privatisations that sold state enterprises as going concerns, whole local authority housing stocks might have been made available by selling shares in new housing trusts or companies. Instead, the approach grew out of earlier practice in selling council housing, and was designed to encourage home ownership rather than any form of private ownership.

The Right to Buy restricted the potential purchaser to the sitting tenant who was neither exposed to market processes nor prices. It offered much larger incentives than available to any other group, and unprecedented levels of discount on market prices skewed tenure choice in favour of home ownership. It increased choices and redistributed benefits, but only to the tenants in the right place at the right time. The value of discounts and the subsequent appreciation of asset value depended on what individual tenants bought, where and when. There was no attempt to achieve any wider measure of fairness among council tenants or between council tenants and others, including homeowners who had paid full market prices for properties. The Right to Buy enabled the government to offer something it felt was electorally popular and relieved councils of responsibilities for repairs, management and maintenance. There was, however, uncertainty about how many sales there would be, where, and with what consequences, and about the impact of reductions in council housebuilding and other housing activity.

These uncertainties did not dissuade the government from adopting the Right to Buy, publicising it, investing effort in ensuring its full implementation across local authorities, and periodically increasing incentives to revive and reaffirm it. Unsurprisingly, the policy had immediate appeal to a significant group of tenants, and this was taken as evidence of its success. Although the government had been reluctant to forecast take-up of the Right to Buy, it is likely that this exceeded expectations. Because purchases were financed by loans from private sector lenders, the immediate capital receipts were much larger than anticipated, although the windfall gain to the Treasury was not reinvested in housing.

After 35 years it is possible to consider the success of the Right to Buy experiment. Some 2 million tenants purchased their home under the scheme, but the extraordinary discounts were only available once for each property – so they initially expanded home ownership, but failed to sustain that growth, and some 40% of Right to Buy properties were transferred to private renting. Governments have been faced with increasing Housing Benefit costs associated with tenants paying market rents in the private sector because there was too little public and social rented housing available.

The wider package of policies introduced alongside Right to Buy also failed to maintain the levels of new building and investment in maintaining the condition and quality of older housing, associated with the previous two-tenure approach to housing. The private sector failed to build the new housing required to fill the gap vacated by reduced local authority activity. Without measures to reinvest capital receipts, and in spite of increased housing association activity, housing shortage re-emerged across the UK. New construction never recovered to 1970s levels, and fell far short of what was needed to meet demographic change let alone rising aspirations. A shortage of housing, of social rented housing and problems of access to home ownership were associated with debate about present and future generations for whom private renting would be the norm, and evidence of increasing overcrowding, sharing and living in sub-standard accommodation. The growing evidence of unhealthy and inappropriate housing alongside escalation of house prices at the top of the market was indicative of the failure of the experiment.

Thirty-five years on, the Right to Buy forms part of the explanation for more severe housing problems and a housing crisis. There has been too little building, too little social housing to meet need or demand, and there is too little local capacity to address problems of access, affordability and housing stress. In the absence of a strategy to rebuild public and social rented housing supply, public expenditure on Housing Benefit is likely to continue and increase without generating the levels of investment in the housing stock that were achieved from earlier expenditures. Local authorities have insufficient housing to meet the demands from homeless and vulnerable households, and are exporting their problems to the private sector and to other districts.

This book sets out the story of the Right to Buy, and the extent to which it represents a strategic policy failure and a preoccupation with short-term political advantage and financial opportunism at the expense of long-term housing objectives. The prospects for new and vulnerable households and the badly housed are worse in 2016 than they were in 1979, and the shortage of public and social rented housing is evident across most of the UK. While governments in Scotland and Wales have recognised problems and taken steps to terminate the Right to Buy, in England there is a determination to ignore the evidence and further extend the policy. The divergence in housing policy within the UK is likely to result in very different patterns of benefit and difficulty. In England, the extension of Right to Buy to housing association tenants is likely to be hailed as a policy success because of a short-term growth in home ownership. But in the long term, the effects of this new phase are likely to be similar to earlier phases: increased home ownership is unlikely to be sustained without continuing subsidies; the extension of the Right to Buy seems likely to destabilise many housing associations and reduce their contribution to housing investment; and the policy involves further dismantling the council sector and incurring an immediate loss of relets in order to finance discounts and replacement building. In 2016, policy in England is still preoccupied with expansion of home ownership rather than any broader-based vision for the housing sector as a whole.

Outline of the book

This book addresses a highly topical issue following government proposals to further extend the Right to Buy in England. It provides an up-to-date account of the origins and precursors of the Right to Buy, the periodic modifications made to the policy, and the evidence about its impact and consequences – intended and unintended. It builds on previous research-based accounts (see, for example, Forrest and Murie, 1990a; Jones and Murie, 2006), and reflects on these in the light of the passage of time. It provides a descriptive account of what the Right to Buy policy is, how it developed and what has happened as a result of it. It captures debates associated with the policy, and discusses current proposals to extend the Right to Buy. Finally, it considers how the proposals to extend the policy in England are likely to affect future housing provision, and what the alternatives are.

The book addresses a series of key debates related to the Right to Buy. Chapter Two sets out the precursors and preconditions for the policy. The Right to Buy has only had so much significance because the UK had, over the 60 years before 1979, built up an unusually large stock of public housing largely owned by local government. There had always been debate about whether this stock should remain in public ownership, and this increased as the sector grew and its finances matured. From the 1950s onwards governments gave general consents for local authorities to sell council houses in England and Wales, and latterly in Scotland and Northern Ireland. The practices and commitments developed in this period shaped the approach to privatisation that followed.

Chapter Three describes how the Right to Buy policy introduced in 1980 broke with the past by removing local discretion and introducing much higher discounts. It refers to the differences in policy adopted in England, Scotland, Wales and Northern Ireland, and to the position of housing association tenants.

Chapter Four presents statistics on the volume of Right to Buy purchases, variations over time and between property types and places, and refers to levels of discount and capital receipts.

Chapter Five offers a commentary on the Right to Buy, referring to its uneven impact, winners and losers, problems and longer-term effects. This final aspect draws on the most recent research about transfers of Right to Buy property to private renting, and the financial implications of this for government.

In view of the measures taken to extend the Right to Buy to housing association tenants in England, Chapter Six discusses the initial proposals put forward during the 2015 general election, the response to these and the agreement reached with housing associations. It discusses the possible consequences of this extension of the policy for council as well as housing association dwellings.

The conclusions presented in Chapter Seven refer to the experience of the Right to Buy over 35 years, to consideration of proposals for their extension, and to alternatives to the continuation and extension of the Right to Buy.

2
SELLING PUBLIC HOUSING: PRECURSORS AND PRECONDITIONS

Introduction

This chapter outlines the origins of public sector housing and its critical role in the improvement of housing supply and housing conditions in in the UK after 1919. It grew to house almost one in every three households in the UK, and this made the potential reach of privatisation considerable. The chapter also outlines debates and the development of policy and practice in selling council properties before the introduction of the Right to Buy in 1980 – and suggests that these helped shape the direction of subsequent housing privatisation.

Building and selling council houses before 1951

The origins of public housing in the UK are rooted in 19th-century legislation, but before the introduction of Exchequer subsidies in 1919, few municipal dwellings had been built. Accounts of public health and housing policy before 1919 refer to a plethora of legislation, but little council housebuilding. Merrett (1979, pp 19-20) refers to three legislative periods leading up to 1914. In the first (1851-75) it became possible for local authorities to build lodging houses within which accommodation was communal. In the second period (1875-

90) powers to build council housing were used, but the costs of compensation and construction presented too great a challenge to most councils. It was in the third period, from 1890 onwards, that most municipal dwellings were built, before 1914.

The Housing of the Working Classes Act 1890 provided the legislative basis for the development of council housing, and the Housing and Town Planning Act 1909 enabled local councils to declare town planning schemes related to specific areas of new development and provided powers that facilitated the building of council dwellings. There was, however, no obligation placed on councils to build, and no financial help from central government to help bridge the gap between costs and the rents that working-class tenants could afford. Some local authorities were also convinced that their intervention in the market would adversely affect the contribution of the private sector: providing municipal housing with subsidised rents would make housing problems worse. Consequently, many local authorities chose not to build council housing. They had concerns about the effect of municipal activity (whether subsidised or not) on private investment in new building, on the housing market and on wages, and about the problems of letting such dwellings at affordable rents in the absence of subsidy other than through providing subsidised land or rate borne subsidy. Where economic and transport development involved demolition of slum or other housing, local authorities rarely embarked on major activity to build replacement housing. Against this background Merrett (1979) concludes that in spite of their extensive powers, local authorities had only built some 100,000 dwellings by 1915.

The change in approach to housing policy after 1919 is detailed in Marian Bowley's seminal account (1945). This describes the shift from a sanitary approach to dealing with existing unhealthy housing, to a series of experiments involving more or less generous central government subsidy, to enable local authorities to build council housing. Different subsidies were provided under legislation in the interwar years, with the emphasis moving to slum clearance rehousing and addressing overcrowding. Changes in rent accounting in 1935 (rent pooling) and powers to provide rent rebates enabled council housing to develop further and to provide housing at more affordable rents for some less well paid workers, although not the lowest paid, people in insecure employment, or unemployed people. While the response of the local authorities was uneven, over 1 million council houses were built in England between 1914 and 1938 (Forrest and Murie, 1988, p 35). Council housing had become part of the landscape of British towns and cities and competed with private renting, especially to house households that wanted higher quality, modern dwellings than were available in most of the private rented sector, and could afford council rents that were generally higher than controlled private sector rents.

Home ownership was promoted alongside council housing and grew much faster in the interwar years – aided by national legislative measures, the growth of building societies and the sale of formerly private rented housing. There were still critics who regarded state participation in the housing market as undesirable, and local authorities that were unenthusiastic about having a continuing role in managing property. Lund (2016) also refers to the Geddes Committee's recommendation for 'a vigorous policy of sale' of council houses as part of an approach to reducing public expenditure. The fact that this did not emerge seems more likely to relate to the practical difficulties of selling at a reasonable price, rather than deep-seated political support for council housing. It is not surprising, however, that some local authorities explored the powers that existed to sell the council housing they had built.

Throughout the interwar period, legislation enabled the sale of council houses subject to the consent of the appropriate minister, the Minister of Health. One of the few references to how these aspects of legislation operated is to active attempts to sell houses by Birmingham City Council (O'Carroll, 1994). Its sales included houses the municipality had built for sale (under the 1923 Act) to sell to households on relatively low incomes. Although households would need to earn more to buy than to rent, applicants to buy were vetted in a similar way to potential tenants, and the conditions attached were similar to those for a tenancy.

Sales of these dwellings were targeted at tenants, households on the waiting list and those in housing need. The Birmingham Municipal Bank, established in 1919, facilitated purchase of municipal housing by tenants (Hilton, 1927). Under the scheme adopted in 1923 tenants were offered their houses at market value, but needed to find 20% of the value as a deposit (with the Municipal Bank advancing 80%). Subsequently, in order to popularise the scheme, lower deposits were required, and by 1925, a special arrangement enabled sitting tenants to become owners on payment of 1% of the purchase price. The weekly commitments associated with purchase of a non-parlour type house were 22s 6d in the first year (Body, 1928, p 93), and this was considerably more than municipal rents, which themselves were unaffordable for many potential applicants and high compared with most of the private rented sector still subject to rent controls. Hilton (1927) refers to 2,422 mortgages effected by the Municipal Bank by 31 March 1927 to enable tenants to become owner-occupiers (out of a total of 6,767 arranged by that date). It is unclear whether these were all sitting tenant purchases, but the figure is consistent with the 3,604 municipal dwellings referred to as having been sold by 1939 (City of Birmingham, 1939).

There are no national statistics on the numbers of council houses sold in this era of occasional sales, but references to local activity include a largely unsuccessful scheme of sitting tenant sales first mooted in Wolverhampton in 1925 and introduced in 1928 (Jones, 1969, p 317), and completed sales recorded in Worcester (Richmond, 1979) Bristol (Bassett, 1980b) and Oxford (Murie, 1975, p 55). O'Carroll (1994, pp 285-6; 1996) refers to a scheme developed by Edinburgh in 1925. Her conclusion, that this scheme foundered because prices were too high (and higher than rents), and the Board of Health was unwilling to approve sales at low prices that would increase deficits, seems likely to apply elsewhere. Edinburgh's revised scheme in 1932 had some success but involved selling vacant units to anyone irrespective of housing need and at lower prices, and there were continuing tensions with the Department of Health over sale prices.

Between the wars the stock of council dwellings that could have been available for sale was small, and historic cost or outstanding debt was high. Where local authorities wanted to encourage sales, market value pricing (or pricing set at, or above, historic costs) would often mean properties were too expensive to buy. Access to loans was also restricted and unsupported by the kinds of favourable deposit and lending procedures that were commonplace at much later dates. Compared with more recent practice, banks and building societies in this period adopted cautious approaches to lending. It seems likely that ministerial consent would be refused if sales were seen to increase deficits in local authority housing accounts. Sales of council houses were limited, and included sales of vacant or built for sale property. The small numbers of sitting tenant sales were likely to have been only to the most affluent tenants and without any significant 'subsidy' in the form of price reduction or discount. Even the occasional sales in the interwar period were halted by wartime restrictions, and Labour governments between 1945 and 1951 rejected the occasional appeals to allow sales, generally referring to outstanding housing problems (Murie, 1975).

Discretionary sales, 1952-79

While other parts of the welfare state were radically changed after 1945, the formula that had improved the housing situation between the wars was retained: subsidies made available to local authorities to build modern, high-quality housing. The subsidies were increased and a system of licensing for new private building ensured that resources available for housebuilding (limited because of wartime measures and slowly increasing subsequently) were mainly channelled to council housing. Aneurin Bevan, as Minister for Health with responsibility for housing, articulated an egalitarian and redistributive role for high-quality council housing to ensure that the housing problems of the working class as well as the middle class were addressed. Local authorities and new towns would have the key role because they could be relied on to plan, implement and sustain a housing programme.

Although this period is the one in which public policy placed greatest reliance on council housing, there were no proposals to nationalise private housing or any part of it. A mixed tenure or mixed economy of welfare approach was maintained, and no attempt was made for housing to adopt the principles of universalism and uniformity associated with other parts of the expanded welfare state, including health, education and national insurance. Public sector housing would play a greater role and ensure overall housing conditions improved, but it would not be the dominant tenure nationally. It is also important to acknowledge continuing debates within government and within the Labour Party about housing tenure. Lund (2016) refers to Labour Party advisers, in the 1940s, suggesting that enabling council house tenants to purchase their homes would be electorally advantageous once the housing shortage was over. Such advice would no doubt have had a mixed reception, begged questions about sale prices, and did not imply immediate action. Periodic questions in Parliament, between 1945 and 1951, urging government to allow council house sales, were met with refusal.

The Conservative government elected in 1951 promoted both council and private housebuilding. It reduced standards, relaxed licensing and controls, and successfully achieved increased housing completions. The rules governing sales of council houses were also changed with provisions in the Housing Act 1936 being replaced in the Housing Act 1952, which repealed the requirement that local authorities obtain the best price at sale, granted the power to limit the price at which a house could be resold or let for up to five years after disposal, and enabled the local authority to reserve to itself the right of pre-emption in the event of any proposal by the purchaser to sell or lease within the five-year period. Following the Housing Act 1952, the Minister for Housing and Local Government provided a general consent for council house sales (MHLG, 1952). This was the first of a series of general consents between 1952 and 1979 that offered a general perspective (sometimes cautious and sometimes encouraging), set out the terms that sales would have to embrace (sale prices and any discounts that could be envisaged), and enabled local authorities to carry out sales and notify the minister on completion (Murie, 1975).

Circular 64/52, issued in August 1952, remained in place until 1960 through a period of Conservative government, but had limited impact. By 1959 some 31% of local authorities had sold just over 13,000 dwellings. But in this period the share of municipal housing continued to grow, and high levels of private construction and disinvestment in the older housing stock by private landlords had increased opportunities to buy elsewhere. There was no appetite to encourage council house sales through subsidies or grants to reduce purchase prices. Enabling local authorities to decide whether to sell, when the resulting rate of sale was modest, was not seen as contentious. Lund (2016) has pointed out that at the 1959 general election it was Labour that included reference to the sale of council houses in its election manifesto. Although no detail was provided, the manifesto stated that 'every tenant, however, shall have a chance first to buy from the council the house he lives in.' Labour, at this stage and subsequently, saw the electoral appeal of home ownership as much as the Conservatives, and competed to be the champions of that tenure.

In view of the importance of sale prices in the interwar history of council house sales and after 1979, it is relevant to note that the general consent continued to emphasise achieving an appropriate price for the sale of an asset. While this did not need to be the best price, it should not represent a give-away. For newer dwellings (built since May 1945) the minimum sale price should be not less than the all-in cost of the dwelling; for older properties, where applying this minimum could imply a price well below current values or returns on rent, the minimum stipulated was not less than 20 times the net unrebated rent. In all cases the local authority should also require that any resale within five years was at a price not in excess of sale price plus an allowance for improvement and with a right of pre-emption precluding sale, grant or lease within five years, unless it had refused the offer to purchase. These stipulations did not make council housing affordable to buy: the historic costs associated with the council housing stock were still high, especially for the substantial volumes of new housing built after 1945.

Circular 64/52 was withdrawn from 1 March 1960 and replaced by Circular 5/60 (MHLG, 1960), which renewed but amended the general consent and formed the basis for decisions until 1967. The new Circular introduced requirements to prevent sales at unreasonably low prices and to bring pricing processes into line with those for compensation. The most important changes, related to pricing, remained consistent with continuing to avoid give-away prices and profiteering.

The new arrangements reflected the ageing or maturing of the local authority stock, which, by 1967, included a larger percentage having market and rental values in excess of historic costs. The new arrangements referred to the need to recognise the value of properties as well as outstanding costs, in setting prices. The Circular stated that, although municipal houses were one of the ratepayers' most valuable assets, sales below market values could be justified and prices were a matter of judgement. The general consent referred to minimum prices that would guard against loss. For dwellings built since May 1945 this would be not less than the capital cost: but this level should not be regarded as the norm, and price should be guided by gross value, and be 35 or 40 times gross value. For older properties the minimum level to guard against loss was likely to be not less than 20 times the net unrebated rent, but again, this should not be regarded as the norm, price should be guided by gross value, and be 35 or 40 times gross value. The stipulations related to resale and pre-emption remained.

Under the terms of the general consent of 1960, sales by local authorities increased but settled between 3,500 and 5,000 between 1961 and 1967. Some 46,000 council houses had been sold in England and Wales between 1951 and 1967, including over 10,000 that had been built for sale (Murie, 1975, p 57). In the same period both municipal housing and owner-occupation expanded rapidly through new construction and transfers from private renting.

The new Labour government of 1964 proposed to increase the role of local authorities in housebuilding and to expand home ownership.

The government favoured sales of dwellings owned by New Town Development Corporations in order to achieve social and economic balance, reformed the leasehold system to grant leaseholders the right to purchase freeholds or extend leases by 50 years, and chose not to withdraw or revise the general consent on council house sales. Between 1964 and 1967 the Labour government accepted local authorities' wish to sell council houses, but they 'should have regard to the value of the capital asset of which they are disposing' (House of Commons Debates, 1965).

The government considered that local authorities ought not to sell their houses where there was an unsatisfied demand for houses to let at moderate rents, and where they intended to continue a substantial programme of building houses to let. Encouragement of home ownership was seen as primarily a matter for the private sector. While the volume of council house sales was low, there was no threat to the government's housing programme, and no actions were needed that would reduce local autonomy or appear inconsistent with ambitions to expand home ownership.

The major shift in debate concerning council house sales arose in the second half of the 1960s and was affected by a number of changes. As Table 2.1 indicates, by 1961 one in every four households lived in council housing in Great Britain, and over 1 million council dwellings were over 20 years old, with a historic debt eroded by inflation.

The finances of council housing had changed and there was scope to sell some older dwellings at a price above historic cost – although controversy remained about what price was appropriate. But more importantly, there was a shift in support for municipal activity associated with increased Conservative control at a local level and with changes within the Conservative Party. Labour control of local authorities declined between 1966 and 1969, especially in urban areas where housing need was greatest. But the effects of this change was greater than in the past because the new Conservative leadership of some councils had a different attitude to council housing than some of their predecessors. This is illustrated in Birmingham where the approach to council house sales was affected by a shift in the balance

Table 2.1: Housing tenure in Great Britain until 1981 (% of dwellings)

Date	Owner-occupied	Rented from		Total number (000s)
		Council, new town or housing association	Private landlord	
Late 19th century[a]	<10	<1	>90	
1914[a]	10-15	1	84-89	
1939	33.0	10.3	56.7	11,500
1953	34.5	18.8	46.6	12,745
1961	44.4	24.3	31.3[b]	14,545
1971	50.6	30.6	18.8	19,000
1981	57.7	31.2	11.1	21,096

Notes: [a] Estimates for England and Wales; [b] housing associations included with private rented.
Source: Pooley, (1992, p 84); Holmans (1987, pp 169-70); Wilcox (2011)

within the Conservative Party away from the Unionist wing, associated with Joseph Chamberlain and taking pride in the tradition of municipal innovation and enterprise, and towards the Conservative wing (Sutcliffe and Smith, 1974; Murie, 1975, pp 75-7). The Conservative group that gained control of the council in 1966 introduced the sales policy that had been promised consistently in manifestos since 1959 and in most years since 1951. Birmingham was one of a number of councils that adopted a more aggressive and evangelical approach to council house sales. The Conservative leader of Birmingham City Council spoke enthusiastically in favour of council house sales at Conservative Party conferences in 1967, 1971 and 1973, and his pamphlets, 'How to sell council houses' (1967) and 'Selling more council houses' (1971), were both published by the Conservative Political Centre and proved very popular. Bassett (1980a) refers to other councils and leaders promoting council house sales at this time – especially the Greater London Council, which also pioneered and publicised council house sales policy.

The Labour government, committed to encouraging owner-occupation, had been content to continue with the existing general consent as long as the volume of sales was moderate. But new Conservative control of local government changed this: local policies changed and council house sales completions shot up. In response, in April 1967 the government issued a new general consent (MHLG, 1967). The preamble contained an implied criticism of local authorities that had expanded sales significantly, even though there was unsatisfied demand for houses to let at moderate rents, and where sales could have an impact on rent pooling and on rates and rents. Local authorities were expected to consider a range of factors and sales should not be substantial in areas experiencing housing pressures. Although the new general consent did not introduce any direct restrictions on local autonomy, it included new guidance about sale prices: for the first time these were to be based on current market valuation. Where there were no restrictions on resale, the full vacant possession market value should determine the price, but where there were restrictions on resale, it would be reasonable to reduce prices by up to 20% below that market value. Although the timing of this general consent was affected by increased local sales activity, it seems likely that a move towards market-related pricing would have been under consideration in any event.

In spite of ministerial exhortations, the number of council houses sold doubled in 1968 and, after asking for monthly reports from authorities embarking on the policy, the minister issued a new general consent in 1968 (MHLG, 1968), replacing that of 1967. Circular 42/68 expressed the view that the sale of council houses were not an intelligent method of encouraging owner-occupation, was financially and socially unwise if pursued unchecked, and mass sales of council houses would seriously affect the ability of local authorities to meet needs as this depended on a regular supply of relets and new construction. Circular 42/68 renewed the general consent with restrictions on the volume of sales: local authorities in the four major conurbations of Greater London, Merseyside, South East Lancashire and the West Midlands were limited to selling one-quarter of 1% of their council housing stock annually.

After 1967 the Conservative Party nationally endorsed local authorities' promotion of council house sales as 'the shop windows' of the Party (Bassett, 1980a). It broke the cautious stance that emphasised the need for housing to let at moderate rents, saw it as a way to both expand home ownership and break up 'huge municipal domains' and prevent 'the extension of state monopoly landlordism' (Murie, 1975; Forrest and Murie, 1998). The differences between the two leading political parties on council housing and council house sales were being widened and emphasised. However, it remains the case that the overall housing strategies continued to envisage new investment in public sector housing, urban renewal and other measures to address problems associated largely with older private sector housing, and measures to subsidise and promote home ownership.

The housing policies adopted by the Conservative government elected in 1970 involved a more residual approach to public sector housing. The Housing Finance Act and Housing (Financial Provisions) (Scotland) Act 1972 removed local authority discretion in setting rents and granting rebates. In England and Wales council rents were to be linked to the 'fair rents' introduced for private tenancies by the Rent Act 1965. These 'fair rents' were the estimated market rents that dwellings would command if supply and demand were broadly in balance in the area in which they were situated. For the first time, rent paid by council tenants would not be related to the cost of providing, managing and maintaining council housing. This marked the most complete change in policy since the introduction of Exchequer subsidies in 1919, and aroused furious opposition. By increasing rents to a level that bore no relation to the cost of provision, the government planned to reduce subsidies and place welfare costs on tenants collectively. Protection for tenants unable to afford market prices would be provided by a national scheme of rent rebates and allowances – replacing the local rent rebate schemes that, in 1964, were only operated by some 40% of housing authorities (Parker, 1967, p 42).

These changes had important implications for council house sales. Because subsidy would in future be based on the overall deficit on the Housing Revenue Account (HRA) rather than calculated from the numbers of council dwellings and when they were built, there was no longer a subsidy (associated with an individual property) that would be suspended in the event of its sale. Instead, the proceeds from the sale reduced the outstanding debt to be serviced. This reduced the Treasury's obligations in respect of housing subsidy, and increased the prospect of payments from local authorities to the Exchequer in the event of a surplus. While the principled considerations relating to disposal at below market value were unaltered by this change, the accounting consequences of selling council dwellings – for both central and local government – had changed. Looked at through this narrow lens there could be short-term advantages associated with council house sales that had not existed previously. For tenants not entitled to rent rebates, the prospect of increasing real rents also meant that the costs of renting would bear a less favourable comparison with the cost of buying the same house on the terms set out by government.

The Conservative manifesto for the 1970 general election stated, 'we will encourage local authorities to sell council houses to those of their tenants who wish to buy them' (Conservative Party, 1970, p 18), and the newly elected Conservative government quickly removed the restrictions on sales introduced in 1968. A new general consent encouraged all local authorities to sell council houses, to 'encourage the spread of home ownership and to increase the opportunities for tenants of council houses to own the houses in which they live' was issued. It reverted back to the terms of the general consent of 1967 with its arrangements for valuation and pricing.

While this general consent remained in place, legislation in 1973 enabled the minister to authorise or require local authorities to control resale for a period of over five years. This addressed fears that purchasers would make a quick profit from buying and selling on. To take account of any extended pre-emption and related conditions, the minister indicated that he would consider individually any applications, falling outside the general consent, that proposed larger reductions in market value (up to 30%). The enthusiasm for council house sales also resulted in the general consent being extended to Scotland.

The number of council houses sold increased from under 7,000 in 1970 to nearly 46,000 in 1972, but then declined in spite of concern expressed by the government (DoE, 1972) and encouragement for local authorities to exercise their powers. This fall was marked in new towns where there was no discretion in implementing policy, and was associated with wider economic, housing market and interest rate changes rather than obstruction by recalcitrant local authorities. House price inflation had taken the value of some dwellings beyond a level that tenants wishing to buy could afford or were willing to pay, and soaring interest rates further eroded demand.

Nevertheless, opinions were increasingly expressed that the government should make it obligatory for local authorities to facilitate tenant purchase. Much of this was directed at Labour councils, but there was also criticism of Conservative-controlled councils that chose not to sell their council housing. By 1973 much of the earlier caution over both purchase prices and restrictions was put aside. Increasing reference was made to the 'right to buy', and decreasing reference to safeguards for the local authority. In addition, some local authority representatives were demanding increased discounts for purchasers.

The Conservatives were out of government between 1974 and 1979, but it is important to recognise that their Right to Buy policy was largely in place in 1974 – their defeat in 1974 delayed rather than acted as the catalyst for the policy. The idea of a Right to Buy had been included in a Private Members' Bill in 1973, and the Conservative Party manifesto of February 1974 stated that, 'in the future, established council tenants would be able, as of right, to buy on reasonable terms the house or flat in which they live' (Conservative Party, 1974a). The intention was to limit the autonomy of local authorities: the number of new homeowners would have been still larger had certain councils not opposed the sale of council houses to those council tenants who were willing and able to buy them with the help offered by the government. The Conservatives, in the October 1974 general election, reiterated the promise of legislation to provide council tenants of three or more years' standing with the Right to Buy at one-third less than market value, with a five-year pre-emption. The Right to Buy, introduced in 1979 and strongly associated with Thatcherism, had been adopted before Margaret Thatcher became leader of her party. Lund (2016) shows that Thatcher, as Shadow Environment Minister, was, at this stage, opposed to council house sales on generous terms – wary of alienating households that had saved and made sacrifices to buy without a large capital sum from the government.

In the last years of Conservative government, high interest and mortgage repayment rates had led to declining housebuilding and a faltering housing market. The rate of council house sales declined and, even if it had been so inclined, there was no need for the new Labour government to restrict sales. In March 1974 it reissued the general consent to sell council houses with a stern refutation of its predecessor's advice, but with no change in the terms involved (DoE, 1974). This general consent remained in place until 1979. The government introduced a rent freeze (in March 1974) and restricted council rent increases as part of its approach to prices and incomes and the management of the economy.

The Housing Rents and Subsidies Act 1975 restored local authorities' power to fix 'reasonable rents', but retained the mandatory rent rebate scheme. A new subsidy scheme used the subsidy level operating in 1975 as the base for subsidy calculation, and retained the principle of a single unified deficit subsidy related to costs incurred. The priorities for action in 1974 were associated with the problems facing builders and developers, and the government enabled local authorities to buy over 9,000 new, unsold properties from private developers. This, along with the municipalisation of older houses and continued new council housebuilding, sustained the expansion of the public sector. Alongside this, the government continued to promote home ownership through tax reliefs and other measures and policies directed at older private housing (Turkington and Watson, 2015) were effective in expanding working-class home ownership.

Lund (2016) draws on various sources to show that Labour in government considered plans to increase council house sales: the policy had electoral appeal and might help to improve labour mobility. Plans were drawn up that involved different arrangements for determining sale prices, but these did not comprise a Right to Buy and would remain subject to local decisions. It is likely that they also assumed that sales would continue to be funded by local authority mortgages, and so capital receipts flowing from them would be limited. In view of Labour's desire to promote home ownership, its acceptance of moderate levels of council house sales and the Conservatives' outstanding commitment to a Right to Buy, it is not surprising that the Labour government re-examined its approach to selling council houses. The public statements of ministers, however, were consistently cautious, and the discussion in the Housing Policy Review (DoE, 1977) reiterated the view that decisions about council house sales should be taken in the light of overall local housing situations.

Whatever its internal deliberations, the Labour government between 1974 and 1979 emphasised the need for affordable rented housing in areas of housing shortage, but left local housing authorities to decide on council house sales. As local electoral fortunes changed, however, more Conservative-controlled councils adopted policies that generated increased sales. By 1977 sales were higher than had triggered the introduction of restrictions nine years earlier. In 1978, sales more than doubled again – to the third highest figure ever. In response, a new general consent was issued in March 1979, in the last months of the Labour government, to prevent sales of empty houses and to restrict sales to tenants of two years' standing or more.

The period of discretionary sales did not end with the election, in May 1979, of a Conservative government committed to introducing a Right to Buy. New legislation would not be on the statute book until October 1980, but the government could and did revise the general consent. In May 1979 a new general consent urged councils to sell dwellings on the terms being proposed in legislation with much larger discounts and lower sale prices. The local elections held alongside the 1979 general election increased Conservative control of the larger housing authorities in England. This, as well as higher discounts and the well-publicised intention to increase rents, provided a compelling package for council tenants to buy, and higher levels of sale were achieved in England in 1979 than in any previous year except 1972 (see Table 2.2), with another new peak in 1980.

The Right to Buy when it was introduced further increased sales, but it is misleading to imply that the default position, had there been no Right to Buy, would have been one of no council house sales. Between 1952 and 1980 over 370,000 public sector dwellings (including properties built for sale) had been sold in England and Wales, with additional sales in Scotland and Northern Ireland (see Chapter Three). Almost a third of this number were sales in 1979 and 1980 under the terms associated with the Right to Buy, but, through much of the 1970s, annual sales under discretionary policies with much lower levels of discount were higher than under the Right to Buy in the period after 1990.

Conclusions

The introduction of the Right to Buy can be explained in different ways and at different levels. More theoretically based accounts refer to the ending of a period in which structural, social, economic and political factors supported collective consumption; they argue that the circumstances favouring the development of public housing were not sustained in a changing local and global economy (see, for example, Harloe, 1985), and that public housing was a temporary stop gap while the private sector adopted new approaches to housing investment to replace failed private landlordism. By the late 1970s, the support for public housing had weakened, and private sector interests had reorganised around home ownership. The expansion of mass home ownership and residualisation of council housing contributed to this change (Murie, 1983; Forrest and Murie, 1983). Other accounts explained failures to sustain the growth of public housing in terms of policies that discriminated against public housing and structural factors favouring home ownership (Kemeny, 1981), or emphasised rents and subsidies, the modernisation of housing policy and policies affecting public housing (Malpass, 1990, 2000).

Table 2.2: Sales of dwellings by public authorities (England and Wales), 1960-80

Year	Local authorities	New towns
1960	2,889	280
1961	3,795	353
1962	4,404	657
1963	3,673	485
1964	3,817	465
1965	3,590	779
1966	4,906	919
1967	4,867	630
1968	9,979	455
1969	8,590	504
1970	6,816	551
1971	17,214	3,438
1972	45,878	16,079
1973	34,334	7,497
1974	4,657	745
1975	2,723	227
1976	6,090	84
1977	13,022	367
1978	30,045	374
1979	41,660	813
1980	81,465	4,231
Total	**334,414**	**39,933**

Source: Housing and Construction Statistics, HMSO Quarterly

Reference is also made to the emphasis on the merits of the market in the ideas of the new right, and neoliberalism. Other accounts refer to how an ageing public sector housing stock, the development of high-rise housing and failures in management and maintenance affected its reputation (van Kempen et al, 2005). Council housing had become more affordable and accessible for poorer households and less attractive to affluent households, and the relative attractiveness of home ownership increased.

Finally, there are international accounts that identify privatisation as a 'shock absorber' rather than an agency of change. At a time of considerable social and political turmoil, ownership of a house symbolised stability and the rewards from an economic system that was more generally associated with uncertainty. For some public sector owners, privatisation was a way of escaping the obligation to address unaffordable maintenance, repair and renewal obligations, and to pass these on to individual households (Jones and Murie, 2006, pp 189-93).

Although all of these explanations have something to offer, this chapter has been less about why privatisation emerged when it did than about the evolution of practices that affected the form it took in the UK. Broader explanations for the loss of support for collective housing do not explain why the privatisation that was to be the major element causing its decline involved a Right to Buy, restricted to sitting tenants becoming homeowners, with distinctive arrangements for pricing and resale. Path dependency was significant in the approach adopted towards privatisation: earlier practice and commitments made by local and national politicians to tenants shaped the Right to Buy.

The 60 years between 1919 and 1979 saw the growth, with cross-party support, of a large public housing sector in the UK. Its share varied between nations and regions, urban and rural areas, but public housing was significant everywhere. By international standards the UK was unusual in having a large public sector and one that was owned and controlled directly by the state rather than through housing associations or other non-government bodies. Most public sector housing was purpose-built family housing, equipped with modern amenities and built to high standards. It was better housing than available to most private tenants and many homeowners. It housed affluent employed households and, until the 1970s, was often beyond the reach of the poorest households. It is because of the size, quality and desirability of the public sector housing stock that the Right to Buy became so important and aroused so much controversy.

The levels of investment in public sector housing in the UK had always been contested, there were always resisters as well as enthusiasts, and there were always suggestions that housing built by the state need not continue to be owned, controlled or managed by the state. The historic debt associated with council housing militated against selling it in the interwar and early postwar years while housing problems and the fear of social disruption associated with inadequate housing, and the crises created during and after two world wars, lent strength to arguments in favour of building and retaining public sector housing. Public housing was a vital part of the formula that had sustained high levels of investment in new housing, replacement of older and sub-standard housing and measurable progress in reducing sharing, overcrowding and slum housing. It had complemented and not replaced a vigorous private sector, and governments had actively promoted home ownership alongside council housing: these two tenures grew at the expense of a poorly managed, poor-quality private rented sector. Investment in public housing was maintained when the economic cycle led the private sector to reduce investment. Where the private sector response to effective demand might not always lead to new supply or improved housing conditions, plans for public sector investment were designed to address need as well as effective demand, and to facilitate slum clearance and gradual renewal. Public sector policies that improved inner-city and other older, poorer quality private housing included acquisition and renewal, but also grants and loans to homeowners, and enabled the private sector to function more effectively.

The history of the sale of council, new town and social rented housing in England goes beyond an account of the legislation and rhetoric emerging from central government or an account of specific or general ministerial consents to selling properties. Whatever general consents were in operation, it was local policy decisions that determined whether or not to sell, who could buy and what would be available for sale. Prior to the Right to Buy there were almost 30 years in which there were general consents for council house sales, and there were a variety of reasons for cautious responses on the part of tenants and local authorities. It is inaccurate to portray all tenants as keen to buy. Taking up the opportunity to purchase was not always possible or attractive because of individual and property factors, access to mortgages, interest rates and wider economic and housing market contexts. It is also inaccurate to portray local decisions to adopt sales policies as simply based on party or political judgements. There were serious issues related to meeting housing need, management and finance. Even where local authorities chose to sell, they made important policy choices in relation to properties that were in very short supply or where management problems were more likely. For example, Conservative councils that adopted policies to sell council dwellings generally excluded some properties – in Birmingham, flats and maisonettes and acquired properties (Murie, 1975), and in Worcester, flats, maisonettes, four-bedroom houses and units for elderly persons (Richmond, 1980).

By the 1970s there was some complacency about the overall housing situation. The promotion of public housing and home ownership had made inroads on housing shortages and problems. At the same time, the failings of some parts of public sector housing were becoming apparent. Older council properties and some multi-storey housing were proving more difficult to let, and the sector was increasingly differentiated in terms of quality, social role and access. There was need for maintenance and renewal in parts of the stock and some estates. Council housing had also adjusted to meet demands, especially from lower-income households who could no longer find housing in the much smaller private rented sector that had previously housed much of this population. The finances of public housing were also maturing – early council estates had little outstanding debt and, therefore cross-subsidised more modern estates. Changes in housing finance and taxation and organisational arrangements favouring home ownership (building societies, estate agents and others) had generated a different political environment and industry around home ownership. By the mid-1970s, the resistance to the sale of council houses was weaker as politicians competed to champion home ownership as the natural form of tenure.

These factors are all relevant to development of the Right to Buy. There was an established tenant population that valued their dwellings, did not want to move, but was attracted by home ownership and regarded rent as wasted expenditure. Politicians could see the opportunity to exploit this. Previous experience had established practices for selling council houses and terms of sale and prices that were attractive to tenants. Attitudes to council housing in both of the major parties were mixed, and paternalistic with traditional approaches more evident than ideological ones. Enthusiasm for selling council housing was related to local political control, but there were Labour councils that chose to sell and Conservatives that refused. Councils had been more or less vigorous builders in the first place, and some had very limited stocks to sell. Some Conservative councils, for example, in rural areas, regarded their small council stock as crucial to meeting local need. The general approach to housing within the Conservative Party, however, shifted away from council housing from the 1950s onwards, and emphasis on home ownership became increasingly strident.

The promotion of council house sales had been pioneered by Conservative local authority leaders rather than the Party nationally. The Conservatives' frustration over the ability of local authorities to resist sales increased along with their willingness to breach local autonomy and local democracy. Electoral calculations also influenced Conservative Party ambitions to break up the concentrations of council house ownership, which were thought to underpin the Labour Party's electoral support in cities. By the 1970s, the Right to Buy had become an exhortation policy linked with uncritical assertions about the merits of home ownership and market processes. Local authorities' reluctance to sell was castigated and associated with socialism and electoral advantage rather than local knowledge or opinion.

3
A POLICY HISTORY OF THE RIGHT TO BUY, 1980-2015

Introduction

The Right to Buy, providing most council tenants with the right to purchase the house they lived in, was to become the most significant privatisation of all those introduced by the Thatcher government. The Right to Buy was regarded by the government as having been a vote winner, and was introduced as part of a package of policies that broke the long established pattern of support for both council housing and home ownership. It was variously regarded as providing neo-Conservative (supporting the family and promoting stability) or neoliberal (increasing reliance on markets) alternatives to the mixed economy of welfare that had operated in the housing sector. It brought the era of management of a housing system with substantial collective ownership to an end – replaced by a market-based deregulated system of housing finance and private renting and subsidised home ownership.

This book argues that the Right to Buy and the wider housing policy package was an experiment in the sense that it sufficiently broke policy continuity, and that its impact was uncertain. There were beliefs that, if councils reduced their housing activity, private actors would flourish and fill the gap, and increasing home ownership would improve decisions about what was built, maintenance and repair and use of the housing stock. But there was no hard evidence to support these beliefs. Indeed, the failure of the market to provide enough appropriate housing, when and where it was needed, partly explained why council housing had developed such a significant role in the UK. There was a real risk that dismantling collective provision would reduce supply and standards and widen housing inequality.

The Right to Buy was also an experiment in privatisation. If housing privatisation had followed the pattern of other privatisations it might have been expected that public housing would have been parcelled up into portfolios of property to be owned and managed by private companies with shares in these companies being sold. Regional or local housing companies might have emerged, as did water companies. But previous proposals for the sale of council houses had accumulated commitments to sitting tenants, and the policy built on the popularity of home ownership. Consequently, only the sitting tenant was given the Right to Buy, and then only to become an owner-occupier. And alongside tax reliefs more generally available to homeowners, Right to Buy purchasers were entitled to unprecedented levels of discount on market prices.

The support to buy was much greater than available to any other group, and sheltered new purchasers from market processes or prices. The policy increased the choices and redistributed benefits to tenants who were in the right place at the right time. The discount formula was applied to an uneven market with very different market values for very similar sizes and types of dwellings in different places. Because of these and other aspects of the Right to Buy experiment, there was uncertainty about how many sales there would be and where, and about the consequences of the policy.

This chapter includes a detailed account of the Right to Buy over its 35 years of operation. In retrospect it was not only the principle of a 'right' to buy that shaped the impact of the policy. Emphasis placed on 'rights' had political and electoral purchase, and this aspect represented an important innovation, breaching previous views that local authorities were best placed to develop local housing strategies and to decide when and where to both build and sell council houses.

But the second innovation, less emphasised in the presentation of the policy, was the unprecedented level of discounts. Over the previous history of council house sales, discounts were justified by constraints on resale, and generally settled at a maximum of 20% of market value. Much more generous discounts were introduced in 1979, and subsequent changes to policy increased these. Levels of discount affected the uptake of the Right to Buy, but also its fairness, value for money and strategic consequences.

First steps

The Conservative manifesto for the 1979 general election emphasised home ownership and the sale of council houses:

> Many families who live on council estates and in new towns would like to buy their own homes but either cannot afford to or are prevented by the local authorities or the Labour government. The time has come to end these restrictions … we shall therefore give council and new town tenants the legal right to buy their homes….

The manifesto went on to refer to the special circumstances of rural areas and sheltered housing for the elderly, discounts ranging from 33 to 50%, and the intention to extend these rights to housing association tenants (Conservative Party, 1979).

In May 1979 the Prime Minister stated:

> Thousands of people in council houses and new towns came out to support us for the first time because they wanted a chance to buy their own homes. We will give every council tenant the right to purchase his own home at a substantial discount on the market price and with 100% mortgages for those who need them. (House of Commons Debates, 1979)

The Housing Act 1980 in England and Wales and Housing Tenants Rights Etc (Scotland) Act 1980 introduced the Right to Buy, and a separate House Sales scheme in Northern Ireland was based on the same model. Other policies to promote low-cost home ownership were developed alongside. There was little attempt to forecast the uptake or impact of the Right to Buy or to set it in the context of other policy ambitions. It was intended to increase home ownership and the government was content to let tenants decide what to do and await the outcome – whatever issues might arise would not weaken their commitment to tenants through the Right to Buy. In responding to the Environment Committee enquiry into proposals for the sale of council houses in 1979 and 1980, the government largely brushed aside issues about the loss of relets, the financial implications of the policy, or whether or not the policy would contribute to the development of welfare housing. These concerns, from the government's perspective, missed the point and the simpler intent of the policy.

The Right to Buy was one of a number of legal rights established for secure tenants, and not subject to local discretion. It applied to almost all secure tenants of three years' standing, and to almost all properties where the landlord was a council, new town, non-charitable housing association or other public sector body (excluding some properties where the public sector landlord did not own the freehold, dwellings built for elderly or disabled people, and some other lesser categories). While the freeholds of houses were to be sold, the sale of flats in England and Wales would be leasehold sales. A statutory procedure for the Right to Buy was designed to limit local variation, and very strong powers were established for the Secretary of State to monitor and intervene in local implementation of the scheme. In line with earlier practice, the base for sale price was a market valuation. Once the valuation was determined, sale prices were calculated to take account of discount and related arrangements. Discounts were based on the number of years of tenancy in any council or other relevant dwelling. They started at 33% (for three years' tenancy), and increased by 1% for each additional year of tenancy up to a maximum of 50%. These rules determined the price unless this meant a discount greater than the maximum cash sum allowed, or unless the price was below the historic cost floor for each property – reflecting outstanding debt associated with construction and any subsequent capitalised repairs.

Procedures in relation to valuation, appeal against valuation, cost floors and maximum discounts were very favourable to the potential purchaser rather than the landlord. In effect, the formula referred to a percentage of value or a cash maximum, whichever was lower, and as long as this did not bring the sale price below the cost floor. In 1980 this maximum cash limit was set at £25,000; it was raised to £35,000 in 1987 and to £50,000 in 1989 and it remained at that level until 1999. Throughout this period no cash limit applied in Scotland. Over time market values and rents changed, but discounts entitlements very rarely approached the maximum discount figure

In practice, purchase prices (and the values of discounts applied) varied enormously depending on where tenants lived and when they bought. An apparently uniform formula to determine purchase price generated very different outcomes. In some cases mortgage repayments very quickly fell below the levels that tenants were paying in rent.

Some other details of the scheme were to have little impact – for example, the legal right to a mortgage, the powers of the Secretary of State to determine procedures for mortgage qualification and the scheme enabling deferred purchase at the current price for up to two years. The requirement for a pro rata repayment of discount in the event of resale within a specified fixed period, initially five years, was more important, and there were detailed conditions relating to dwellings that had been purpose-built for elderly or disabled households, and (largely ineffective) arrangements designed to protect properties in designated rural areas by providing a locality condition or pre-emption clause limiting who could buy on resale. These details can be seen as responses to concerns expressed about sales by Conservative-controlled councils and others. The general intention was to minimise exclusions and to make it very difficult to subvert the purpose of the legislation. The monitoring and interference in local implementation was much more invasive than normal in central–local relations over housing – extending to the appointment of a commissioner in Norwich (Forrest and Murie, 1985). The Right to Buy scheme was a highly publicised exhortation policy, and its attractiveness for tenants was increased because the policy was for rents to rise in real terms.

At this stage it is relevant to note two factors that affected the impact of the Right to Buy. First, the expectation that it would operate alongside a significant programme of council housebuilding was not realised. Michael Heseltine, former Secretary of State for the Environment, celebrating the birth of the Right to Buy, had stated that a council housebuilding programme of 60,000 homes a year would continue (*The Guardian*, 1979), but council house completions in England actually fell from 74,790 in 1979/80 to 74,840 in 1980/81, 54,880 in 1981/82 and to 31,660 in 1982/83. By 1986/87 they were below 20,000 (DCLG, Live Tables, Table 209). Second, the volume of immediate capital receipts associated with the Right to Buy was much greater than expected. Under discretionary sales policies most mortgages appear to have been provided by local authorities, which effectively replaced one debt with another that would be paid off, and yield receipts, slowly. In the event, the proportion of Right to Buy sales in England financed by the private sector was 41% in 1981/82, 57% in 1982/83, 70% in 1983/84, 79% in1985/86 and 93% in 1987/88. This pattern meant that public sector debt was transferred much more quickly to the private sector, generating a windfall gain for the government. It also reduced the significance of the Right to a Mortgage.

The failure to achieve higher levels of council housebuilding is particularly significant in view of this pattern of capital receipts. In spite of a windfall financial gain, because of the Right to Buy, the government chose not to address the issue of replacement investment or to address the impact of the projected loss of relets. There was no commitment to use capital receipts for housing. From the start of the Right to Buy, restrictions were placed on the use of receipts – initially limiting councils to using 20% of the receipts they generated from sales and restricting what this could be spent on. In 1990 the government further tightened the limitations placed on local authorities' use of receipts from sales: the Local Government and Housing Act 1989 required local authorities that were not debt-free to reserve 75% of receipts from Right to Buy sales for debt redemption or for paying off credit agreements. The remaining 25% 'usable receipts' could be used as provision for credit liabilities or to finance capital expenditure on any aspect of local authority service. Effectively the bulk of receipts went to the Treasury nationally to be used as the government wished – largely for purposes other than housing.

Strengthening the Right to Buy

The Right to Buy has remained in place in England since 1980 with no government proposing its abolition. In contrast, in Scotland and Wales, actions were taken to abolish it between 2014 and 2016. The policy was perceived as having financial advantages through the generation of capital receipts until the mid-2000s, but by then, economic and housing market circumstances were unfavourable, and the progress of previous sales and stock transfers had reduced its potential impact. The longevity of the Right to Buy was, however, principally associated with its electoral appeal. The Labour Party initially expressed opposition to the Right to Buy because it infringed on local democracy and depleted the supply of rented housing in high demand areas. Labour's manifesto at the June 1983 general election referred to ending the enforced sale of council houses, empowering public landlords to repurchase homes sold under the Tories on first resale, and providing that future voluntary agreed sales would be at market value (see Lund, 2016). Labour did not lose the general election simply because of this opposition, but the view that supporting the Right to Buy was an electoral necessity became accepted wisdom. Labour's opposition was short-lived and, after 1983, both the Conservative and Labour Parties nationally supported the Right to Buy.

Over the next 15 years the Right to Buy was relaunched periodically and enhanced largely to exploit its electoral appeal. Following Conservative victory at the June 1983 general election the Housing and Building Control Act 1984 strengthened the Right to Buy. It tidied up technical details, closed loopholes, provided a right to purchase a shared ownership lease, and extended the Right to Buy to tenants of only two years' standing, with discounts increased from 32% for two years' tenancy to a new maximum of 60% for 30 years. This brought an estimated 250,000 additional tenants within its scope. The Act also included more dwellings for disabled people, and was extended to county councils and tenant successors; some 50,000 additional tenants were included by extending Right to Buy to properties where public sector landlords did not own the freehold, but there were sufficient years remaining on the lease (at least 25 for houses and 50 for flats).

While the Housing Act 1985 further consolidated Right to Buy legislation, the Housing and Planning Act 1986 made changes to further strengthen it. By 1986 it was apparent that sales of flats were lagging well behind the sale of houses – the Right to Buy was not leading to a proportionate sale of flats. The response, through the Housing and Planning Act 1986, was to introduce a differential rate of discount for flats with more rapid progression to a higher maximum. The discount for houses remained at 32% for two qualifying years of tenancy, rising by 1% for each additional year to a maximum of 60% (after 30 years' qualifying tenancy), but discounts for flats started at 44% for two qualifying years and progressed by 2% for each additional year to a maximum of 70% (after 15 qualifying years). The Act also reduced the discount repayment period for all Right to Buy sales from five years to three, and developed the framework for stock transfer, redevelopment and delegation of the management of estates and the provisions to preserve the Right to Buy for tenants whose properties were affected by transfer or similar changes. The higher rate of discount for flats and arrangements for a preserved Right to Buy were retained in all revisions of the Right to Buy after 1986.

Higher discounts for flats further eroded any connection with earlier justifications for levels of discount. Discounts were not seen as compensation for restrictions on resale or as related to length of tenancy, but were explicitly designed to bias tenure choice in favour of purchase and to persuade tenants to buy flats. Ministers presented the policy in the context of the problems of the inner city and the inadequacies of bureaucratic and monopolistic public housing sector.

Policy was designed to dismantle the legacy of council housing and policies for Housing Action Trusts, Tenants' Choice of Landlord and stock transfer to housing associations operated alongside the Right to Buy to achieve this. The approach involved a further shift away from investment in council housing. By 1988 housing associations had shown a willingness to embrace private finance and the Housing Act 1988 introduced assured tenancies and enabled housing associations to use mixed funding to invest in rented housing – a formula preferred by successive governments. Housing associations, as part of the private sector, became an attractive alternative: because of new-found access to private finance, any given level of government grant generated more investment than if the same grants went to local authorities. In view of later debates, it is also salutary to refer to ministerial thinking at the time. William Waldegrave pondered:

> Do we really want the state to build new saleable houses, which it will then sell at a discount? For what? As a way of providing subsidised houses for first-time buyers? That would be a very elaborate way of doing that, and very random in who it helped. (quoted in Murie, 1989)

Housing associations were tasked with the principal role in providing new rented housing partly because they were not obliged to sell at a discount under the Right to Buy. Nevertheless, the commitment fell far short of that indicated in 1979, or needed to replace Right to Buy sales.

Measures affecting the Right to Buy after 1986 were less dramatic but continued to simplify and increase its attractiveness. The Housing Act 1988 introduced compensation for tenants whose landlords were slow in carrying out their duties in relation to the legislation, removed the cost floor for properties more than eight years old and at the same time the maximum cash discount was increased to £50,000. The Leasehold Reform, Housing and Urban Development Act 1993 dispensed with underused and complicating factors (the Right to a Mortgage, deferred completion of purchase and shared ownership leases), and the Housing Act 1996 introduced new measures to provide a Right to Acquire for housing association tenants.

The higher rates of discount introduced in 1986 increased sales of flats but exposed the lack of understanding of leaseholders' rights and obligations among purchasers and their advisers. Ministers were made increasingly aware of disputes and disenchantment related to service charges, and especially the significant bills for leaseholders to pay for major works to properties. The first significant government response came in 1995, when a package of measures to help leaseholders included a good practice guide and making it possible for councils to use mortgage indemnity schemes or an exchange sale scheme (buying back the Right to Buy property at its sale price and selling them another property at up to 40% discount). The Housing Act 1996 allowed the Secretary of State to issue directions for landlords to reduce or waive service charges for repair, maintenance or improvement works. Using these powers, the Housing Minister allowed landlords to reduce or waive charges: where major works were carried out with assistance from specified government programmes, the landlord should charge not more than £10,000 over any five-year period – unless the benefit to the leaseholder exceeded this.

Labour and the Right to Buy, 1997-2010

Although the Right to Buy is associated with governments led by Margaret Thatcher, her successors maintained the policy in England while different approaches emerged in Scotland, Wales and Northern Ireland. The Labour Party, in opposition between 1979 and 1997, had come to terms with the Right to Buy, and become enthusiastic about transferring council housing to housing associations. Although the Labour government elected in 1997 did not immediately change the Right to Buy in England, it honoured its election commitment to release housing capital receipts for reinvestment in new building and repair and improvement of the council stock. The Local Government Finance (Supplementary Credit Approvals) Act 1997 enabled the phased release of reserved receipts from council house sales. Later measures (under the Local Government Act 2003) introduced enabled local authorities to use 25% of receipts for any capital purpose (including buying back Right to Buy properties), with the remaining 75% to be pooled and distributed by central government to enhance capital spending. The sale of council houses continued to provide an alternative source for government to finance policy, and was not hypothecated on housing.

In much the same way that it had dealt with discretionary sales in earlier years, Labour sought to moderate the excesses associated with the Right to Buy. In its comprehensive spending review the government expressed a strong commitment to promoting sustainable homeownership and a wish for the Right to Buy to continue with tenants having the opportunity to buy at generous discounts, but it was concerned to improve value for money from this and other programmes. Following consultation (DETR, 1998a), the government in England made changes to the discount arrangements for the Right to Buy (DETR, 1998b). From February 1999 maximum discounts available to tenants applying to exercise their Right to Buy were reduced from £50,000 to levels that differed between regions, broadly in line with property valuations. The highest ceiling was in London (£38,000) and the lowest in the North East (£22,000) with the East at £34,000, the South West at £30,000, the North West and West Midlands at £26,000 and the East Midlands and Yorkshire and Humberside at £24,000. A maximum cash discount was set for Wales at £24,000. The proposals to improve value for money also resulted in modifications to the cost floor rules to include repair and maintenance costs as well as other costs incurred over a ten-year period (replacing the previous eight years).

At this stage there were attempts to assess the effect of reduced discounts on the uptake of the RTB. Research commissioned by government (Marsh et al., 2003) indicated that many applicants and purchasers were not aware that discount arrangements had changed and that the introduction of new regional ceilings had not affected average discounts significantly. The surge in RTB applications in early 1999 was affected by changes to discounts but other factors, including the general housing market situation and high stock transfer activity (with implications for rents and management) also encouraged applications. A third of applicants withdrew their applications and at the most 46% of these withdrawals could have been affected by discount policy change. Those applicants who went on to complete purchases were asked how much they were willing and able to pay and most indicated that they were willing to pay more than they were actually required to – a proportion of purchases could have proceeded with a lower discount. Although higher discounts would have persuaded some additional applicants to buy the uptake achieved at lower discounts suggested that the very high discounts previously available were unnecessary to achieve sales but had reduced capital receipts.

These changes did not remove concerns about the continuing impact of Right to Buy sales on local housing needs. Growing concern about affordability and housing shortages resulted in a further, selective reduction in the maximum discount in the South of England in 2003 (DETR, 2003). In nine local authority areas in the South East region and in all except two London boroughs, the maximum discount was set at £16,000 rather than the £38,000 figure for London and the South East. One further adjustment to the Right to Buy designed to address rural housing affordability problems was the introduction of restrictions on the resale of Right to Buy homes in the seven National Parks in England, the 37 Areas of Outstanding Natural Beauty and 35 areas that were designated as rural for this purpose. Reductions in maximum discounts reflected a more restrained attitude to the Right to Buy.

A separate public sector value for money calculation carried out by Wilcox (2006) and referring to the costs of loss of relets and lost rental income concluded that any RTB discounts in excess of 32% imposed net costs on the public sector: average discounts in excess of 35% would be likely to impose net long term costs on the public sector, while average discounts constrained to below 30% would be likely to deter sales that represented reasonable value for money for the public sector. While the assessments by Marsh et al (2003) and Wilcox (2006) provide reasonable benchmarks for discussion of appropriate levels of discount they are inevitably open to challenge. In particular rates of turnover and reletting would be likely to be different if tenants had not bought – some tenants would have moved away to buy and so released properties to let. Unfortunately later proposals related to discounts in England attributed declining rates of RTB sales to reduced discounts, asserted the need for higher discounts and failed to build on or refer to earlier calculations and considerations about value for money.

In England the Labour government's stock transfer programme would eventually reduce the potential of the Right to Buy as council tenants transferring to housing associations and entitled to the Preserved Right to Buy were replaced by tenants with neither the Right to Buy nor the Preserved Right to Buy. There is, however, no evidence that this was a significant aim of stock transfer policy, and the purpose was rather to increase investment in social housing by attracting private finance and to change management by transferring ownership to housing associations. The government also appeared to be responding to arguments that Right to Buy capital receipts should be reinvested in new rented housing and the maintenance and improvement of the public sector stock. The Decent Homes policy involved active investment to modernise the remaining public sector housing stock, and there was continued investment in social housing through the Housing Corporation.

Increasing concerns were expressed at this stage about the impact of the Right to Buy on the regeneration of council-built estates (where plans for the major restructuring of estates, including demolition, triggered applications under the Right to Buy that could considerably delay activity and increase costs), and about the activities of companies seeking to exploit the Right to Buy (Jones, 2003; Marsh et al, 2003). The Housing Act 2004 introduced a variety of measures (coming into effect from 18 January 2005) designed to increase value for money and curb abuses by property developers and tenants. Where tenants had entered into agreements to sell their home to a third party before the end of the discount repayment period, they would be required to repay some or all of their discount, as if they had sold their home at the time of the agreement. Where the landlord intended to demolish a property, the Right to Buy could be suspended when an initial demolition notice was served, and ended when a final demolition notice was served.

In addition to other detailed changes (Jones and Murie, 2006), the Housing Act 2004 introduced a more restrictive formula, with the Right to Buy being available to tenants of five years' standing (rather than two). Discounts started at 35% for houses and 50% for flats with progression to maximum percentage discounts unchanged. The period in which the discount had to be repaid in the event of resale reverted to five years (from three), with discretion to waive the requirement for repayment of discount where it might lead to hardship. The amount to be repaid, if the property was sold within five years, would be a percentage of the market value when it was resold disregarding the value of the improvements made by the owner of the property. This legislation also allowed the Right to Buy to be refused to tenants subject to an Anti-Social Behaviour Order, and introduced the right for local authorities to have first refusal if the property was available for sale within 10 years of first being sold.

Throughout their period in government Labour grappled with continuing issues related to leasehold properties. Manifest disaffection among leaseholders had increased as local authorities implemented ambitious programmes to address the backlog of disrepair and bring their stock up to the Decent Homes standard by 2010, in line with the government's strategy. In mixed tenure blocks (council and Right to Buy), leaseholders became liable for their share of the costs of upgrading. The government's response, through the Housing Act 2004, was to strengthen the duty on social landlords to provide information to their tenants about the Right to Buy, including information about service charges that owners of leasehold properties must pay to their landlords. Between 2005 and 2007 the government also carried out consultations about the problems faced by social sector leaseholders (Wilson and Bate, 2015).

The government completed its review in March 2007 (DCLG, 2006). It concluded that only a small percentage of leaseholders were facing very large bills (a survey of 26 London boroughs indicated that just over 9,000 [6%] of 143,000 council leaseholders had major works bills of £10,000 or more). Especially for large blocks of flats, it would be more expensive to carry out piecemeal repairs than to complete comprehensive repairs and improvements at one time. While major works bills would be higher in the short term, the quality of work would be better, and future maintenance costs would be lower.

While more help could be provided for leaseholders faced with large bills, capping all such bills would generate problems and be very expensive – costing more than £40 million in London. Instead, local authorities were urged to inform and advise leaseholders who faced particularly high bills for major works, about payment options: to offer the full range of payment options to help leaseholders pay their bills, to share best practice and to use existing resources to assist leaseholders in hardship. Finally, the Housing and Regeneration Act 2008 enabled local authorities to offer, to leaseholders who bought under the Right to Buy, equity loans for service charge payments and to buy a share in flats by cancelling part or all of the leaseholder's service charge liability (Wilson and Bate, 2015).

Coalition government 2010-15: reinvigorating the Right to Buy in England

By 2010 the Right to Buy had existed for 30 years but operated in a very different context. It applied to a much smaller council housing sector reduced by the Right to Buy itself, stock transfers and low rates of new council housebuilding. Sales had been uneven spatially and in terms of property type, and the profile of tenants and dwellings had changed with a smaller proportion of houses and of affluent households. As the number of council tenancies declined, so did the number of tenants entitled to the Right to Buy. Stock transfers progressively reduced the reach of the Right to Buy as tenants with the Preserved Right to Buy were replaced by assured tenants with no Right to Buy. The largest group of tenants in the social rented sector continued to qualify for the Right to Buy, but what this was worth varied according to property type, place, individual circumstances and property values. Some tenants did not want to buy at all and others did not want to buy the property they currently lived in (Rowlands and Murie, 2008).

Against the background of the credit crunch, economic recession and a massive budget deficit, the Conservative-Liberal Democrat coalition government formed after the election in May 2010 embarked on an austerity agenda that was consistent with Conservative ambitions to reduce the role of the state. The housing package included cuts in capital expenditure that reduced investment in new social housing and housing renewal and regeneration activity, increases in rents and changes in regulatory arrangements. More innovative proposals related to Housing Benefit with new caps on the maximum benefit available to tenants, a 'bedroom tax' that penalised tenants of working age deemed to be under-occupying their dwelling, and limits placed on benefits paid for properties with higher rents. Longer-term proposals saw Housing Benefit forming part of a new Universal Credit system and affected by an overall benefit cap. Policies for social housing departed from the previous emphasis on the rights of secure tenants, and a consultation paper referred to the need for a change:

> Margaret Thatcher introduced statutory lifetime tenure for social housing in 1981. Times have changed, and it is no longer right that the Government should require every social tenancy to be for life, regardless of the particular circumstances.... (DCLG, 2010, p 5)

It was proposed to introduce a new, more flexible affordable rent tenancy for the next generation of tenants. Under the Localism Bill published in 2010, social landlords would, in future, be able to offer more flexible tenancy arrangements to new tenants, and new homeless applicants. And the pressure to work with the government's agenda was considerable: where councils and housing associations decided not to adopt the more flexible affordable rent tenancy, their capacity to finance active development strategies would be affected.

The key Thatcherite privatisation measures in housing had rewarded long-term recipients of subsidised housing with increased tenancy rights, including a Right to Buy. In contrast, the package introduced in 2010 reduced support for many working-age and new tenants, and especially those dependent on benefits, living in high demand areas, having a spare room or staying in the family home as their household shrunk. The approach that had been popular in 1979, when one in three households were council tenants, had less appeal in 2010. In 2010 attacks on the welfare system and those receiving benefits had replaced the populist agenda around tenants' rights. By 2010, rather than rewarding long-term tenants, there were proposals to reduce security. The approach involved attacking existing rights and responding to a view that tenants had it too easy.

While the coalition was dismantling aspects of the legislation of 1980 and emphasising local control over decisions, it did not extend the logic of either of these to the Right to Buy. In October 2011, the Prime Minister announced the intention to resuscitate the Right to Buy, and in November 2011, the government published *Laying the Foundations: A housing strategy for England* (DCLG, 2011). By this time the previous year's cuts were having an effect. In spite of the rhetoric, new construction had fallen, and the affordable housing programme, supported by government subsidy, was in collapse.

The government's housing strategy was presented as a plan to increase housing construction, help local economies and create jobs. The Prime Minister referred to home ownership as something that should be achievable for everyone and policies to encourage home ownership. These included a revived Right to Buy that predictably altered restrictions on maximum discounts, but also included a commitment to use receipts from sales to fund new affordable housing (on a one-for-one replacement basis). The continued enthusiasm for the Right to Buy in England was remarkable for the absence of any reference to value for money or the need to recalibrate the policy in light of a deteriorating overall housing situation, changes to tenants' rights or spending plans and priorities. The next phase in the Right to Buy and the emphasis placed on replacement of sold dwellings was facilitated by changes in the subsidy system for council housing. The Localism Act 2011 abolished the existing HRA deficit subsidy and redistributed outstanding housing debt between councils with retained housing stocks. An overall borrowing limit was established along with other elements to underpin 30 year business plans for local authority Housing Revenue Accounts. Rental income would support efficient and effective housing management and service outstanding debt. Where income was sufficient councils could embark on new investment on a scale commensurate with these resources. In this context it could be possible to replace any properties sold if both the receipts and the resources in the HRA were sufficient.

The Right to Buy was relaunched in England in 2012 (DCLG, 2012) with the same formula linking discount to years of tenancy and the differences between flats and houses (for houses 35% after five years rising by 1% a year to a maximum of 60% after 30 years; and for flats from 50% after five years rising thereafter by 2% a year to a maximum of 70% after 15 years). However, a much higher figure for the maximum discount (£75,000) was introduced across England with no regional differentials. While this could be seen as in the tradition of tinkering with the detail of the Right to Buy to reflect changing government attitudes, there was an important innovation with a commitment to reinvesting capital receipts and replacing the dwellings lost to the social rented sector on a one-for-one basis.

The relaunch of the RTB in 2012 was accompanied by an impact assessment (DCLG, 2012). This referred to lost rental income and increased housing benefit costs but emphasised the effects of increased supply and construction activity associated with the replacement of sold properties on a one for one basis. Questions about the level of discount were side stepped by asserting that reduced discounts accounted for reduced sales after 2003: consequently increased discounts were needed to increase sales. The National Audit Office (2016) highlighted the extent to which a positive assessment of the policy rested on the successful delivery of one for one replacement.

In March 2013, because of increasing property prices and sluggish Right to Buy sales in London, the government further increased the maximum discount available in London boroughs to £100,000 – so reintroducing a regional differential (DCLG, 2013). In the Autumn

Statement 2013 the government announced a £100 million fund to improve access to mortgage finance and to provide agents to guide people through the process of buying. This was followed in January 2014 (DCLG, 2014) by the announcement that the maximum discount for houses would be increased to 70% (in line with flats, but with a slower progression to this level at 1% for each year). From July 2014, the maximum cash figure for discounts would be increased annually, in line with the Consumer Price Index (CPI): by 2015 the discount was £103,900 in London and up to £77,900 elsewhere in England. Finally, the Deregulation Act 2015 included measures (coming into force in May 2015) to reduce the qualifying tenancy period for the Right to Buy from five to three years. Discounts for houses were 33% after three years, rising by 1% a year to a maximum of 70% after 40 years; and for flats, 50% after three years and rising after five years by 2% a year to a maximum of 70% after 15 years.

The impact of this succession of measures is difficult to evaluate. The volume of sales by local authorities in England increased from below 3,000 each year between 2008-09 and 2011-12 and doubled in 2012-13, before almost doubling again in 2013-14. Nevertheless, sales remained lower than in any year between 1981-82 and 2006-07. The low level of sales in 2010 partly reflected the economic crisis and changes restricting access to mortgages. After 2012 there were higher Right to Buy discounts than ever before, increased marketing of the Right to Buy and the effects of the financial crisis were weakening. Nevertheless, Right to Buy sales remained at a very low historic level. How much of the relatively small increase in sales after 2011 is attributable to the relaunch of the Right to Buy rather than a relaxation of wider market constraints is unknown. Assessments of whether the government's commitment to replace properties sold after the discounts were raised were also difficult, if only because there was bound to be a time lag between sale and replacement. New dwelling starts in England by local authorities and housing associations between 2012/13 and the third quarter of 2014/15 were 2,712, considerably less than needed for replacement (Wilson and Bate, 2015).

In the midst of its actions to reinvigorate the Right to Buy, the coalition government faced the perennial problems concerning charges for leaseholders. On coming to office it had decided not to take forward the proposals that the previous government had been considering related to sinking funds. In 2012, however, it allowed local authorities to fund up to 50% of the cost of re-purchasing a former council home, up to a maximum of 6.5% of any additional net receipts. The idea of capping service charges was revived following the case of Florence Bourne, a 93-year-old, given a £49,000 bill for internal and roof repairs by Newham Council. A Leasehold Valuation Tribunal found these charges 'not reasonable', and following consultation two measures were introduced (August 2014) to cap leaseholder service charges (at £10,000 over five years and £15,000 in London) for all work carried out, partly or wholly funded by central government. Mandatory caps applied whatever funding from government was allocated after this date, but only where the property was the leaseholder's principal home. The cap would not apply where leaseholders rented out the property.

Housing associations and the Right to Buy

Although the Right to Buy had generally been couched in terms of the sale of council houses, the Conservative manifesto in 1979 had indicated the intention for it to also apply to housing association tenants. In the event, however, the Housing Acts of 1980 excluded tenants of charitable housing associations because of amendments tabled and passed in the House of Lords (Murie, 2008a). The housing association movement, largely through their trade association, the National Federation of Housing Associations (NFHA), mobilised support in the House of Lords to safeguard the right of charitable organisations to hold their assets in perpetuity. The House of Lords included Conservative peers who were strongly associated with housing associations, including two trustees of the Guinness Trust. They campaigned with their Conservative colleagues to overturn proposals for the Right to Buy to apply to charitable housing associations. The government vigorously resisted but lost the vote. Rather than further delay the legislation or risk another defeat, the government reluctantly accepted this outcome – one that proved very important for the subsequent development of housing associations. The insulation of most of the housing association sector from the Right to Buy further separated it from the municipal rented sector. Tenants of non-charitable housing associations had a right to buy their homes and to obtain a mortgage from the Housing Corporation, but charitable associations were untouched, and many existing and newly formed housing associations (including stock transfer associations) adopted charitable status to avoid corporation tax liability and to benefit from the exemption from the Right to Buy. In 2011/12 it was estimated that 1% of housing association tenants were eligible for the RTB because they were secure tenants and around 25% were eligible for the preserved RTB (Wilson, 2014).

Until 2015 there were no further proposals to make the Right to Buy apply to housing association tenants. There were, however, a number of actions taken to extend opportunities for house purchase to housing association tenants. Various low-cost home ownership measures, introduced in and around 1980, were designed to enable anyone to access home ownership (Malpass and Murie, 1987). After 1980 a complex series of voluntary schemes were specifically targeted at housing association tenants, followed by a statutory scheme in 1996 (Murie, 2008a).

The statutory Right to Acquire, introduced by the Housing Act 1996, operated after 1 April 1997. It conferred a right on eligible housing association tenants living in qualifying properties to buy their home at a discount. It only applied to properties built or acquired by housing associations, both charitable and non-charitable, with public funds, after 1 April 1997. It applied to new build and rehabilitation for rent schemes that received a Social Housing Grant, and tenanted property transferred to a registered social landlord from a public sector landlord from 1 April 1997. Some properties (including sheltered housing and homes located in small rural settlements) were excluded. Tenants eligible for Right to Acquire were entitled to a flat rate grant unrelated to length of tenancy. Almost 4,000 dwellings were purchased under the Right to Acquire between 1998-99 and 2014-15 in England (see Table 3.1).

Table 3.1: Annual sales under the Right to Acquire, England, 1998-99 to 2013-14

Year	Dwellings
1998-99	0
1999-2000	0
2000-01	20
2001-02	40
2002-03	110
2003-04	240
2004-05	410
2005-06	470
2006-07	570
2007-08	540
2008-09	180
2009-10	90
2010-11	200
2011-12	140
2012-13	150
2013-14	240
2014-15	380
Total	3,780

Source: DCLG Live tables, Social housing sales, Table 677

Tenants who did not have the Right to Buy or Right to Acquire were potentially entitled to use the Voluntary Purchase Grant scheme, also introduced in 1996. This did not confer a statutory right or duty, but enabled tenants of charitable as well as non-charitable housing association to purchase the home they lived in at a flat rate discount equivalent to the existing Tenants' Incentive Scheme (TIS), introduced in 1991/92. Social HomeBuy replaced the Voluntary Purchase Grant in

April 2006. This enabled tenants of participating local authorities and housing associations to buy a share of between 25 and 100% in their rented home. Social HomeBuy was regarded as particularly relevant for housing association tenants who did not have the Right to Buy or Right to Acquire, and social tenants who could not afford outright purchase. Tenants received a discount (on the initial share purchased and on any additional shares they bought) equivalent to the Right to Acquire discount (between £9,000 and £16,000, depending on location), pro rata to the share purchased. The evaluation of the pilot scheme suggested that there was little demand for it from tenants with the Right to Buy (Rowlands and Murie, 2008). Between 2006-07 and 2013-14 only 560 dwellings had been sold through Social HomeBuy – 40 by local authorities and 520 by housing associations (DCLG Live tables, Social housing sales, Table 683).

The exclusion of charitable housing associations from the Right to Buy might have been regarded as relatively insignificant in 1980. It affected some 400,000 out of 5.5 million 'social rented' tenants in England. The significance of the exclusion grew with the expansion of housing associations following the adoption of private finance, assured tenancies and then with policies of stock transfer. Essentially the government, while continuing to promote the Right to Buy for public sector secure tenants, was persuaded by housing associations to enable them to access private finance and to let their dwellings as assured tenancies in order to facilitate private lending for housing association development. The attraction of this formula was that for any given level of capital grant to housing associations, the government could achieve a higher level of new building for rent than if the same funding was available to local authorities that were unable to lever in private loans. Government policy favoured the development of housing association-assured tenancies that did not have the Right to Buy, and this formula worked to increase investment in affordable housing at a time when this had become an urgent issue.

Stock transfers from local authorities were stimulated by the same thinking and by the continuing desire to dismantle council housing. The government encouraged local authorities to transfer their stock to housing associations, paying off public sector debt and accessing private finance for refurbishment and new investment in rented housing. Arrangements that made stock transfer compatible with the Right to Buy involved a distinction between the rights of existing tenancies (which had a Preserved Right to Buy) and any tenancies that started after transfer and did not have the Right to Buy. The proportion of tenancies with the Right to Buy declined over time in stock transfer housing associations, while new as well as existing local authority tenants (where stock transfer had not occurred) retained the Right to Buy. The stock transfer process initiated by a Conservative government after 1986 and expanded under Labour after 1997 progressively reduced eligibility for the Right to Buy and expanded housing associations.

Although the Right to Buy did not apply to charitable housing associations, the legislation was used to sell almost all of the small co-ownership or nascent cooperative sector. In Great Britain the government had promoted co-ownership housing through the Housing Corporation, and between 1961 and 1980 some 40,000 co-ownership dwellings were built with residents collectively owning the assets, following development through a co-ownership society. The early 1980s saw the dismantling of this sector. Powers to dispose of properties, with the Housing Corporation's consent, were included in the Housing Act 1980, and facilitated the sale of co-ownership dwellings.

For the individual co-ownership purchaser, the terms of sale that emerged were enormously attractive as all that was required was to clear the outstanding loan and any other debts. Effectively it was a sale at historic cost, well below the market price: no account was taken of the use that had been made of government funds or other support, and sales did not generate the capital receipts that they could have. By the time of the Housing Act 1980 there were around 900 co-ownership and co-ownership equity sharing societies. Over 70% of societies had received approval to sell up by the end of March 1982, and over 90% by 1990/91. Applications from societies to the Housing Corporation for permission to proceed with sales, between 1980/81 and 2008/09, show a total of 861, with 860 completed (Murie, 2008a).

Right to Buy in Scotland, Wales and Northern Ireland

There were always local and regional variations in the operation of discretionary policies for the sale of council dwellings, and differences in Scotland and Northern Ireland reflected the devolution of housing powers well before 1998. However, the new devolved governments established in Scotland and Wales and Northern Ireland in 1998 adopted new approaches to the Right to Buy (see also Parkin, 2015).

Scotland

Before 1979 the demand for discretionary house sales policies was less evident in Scotland than England. In the postwar period, housing in Scotland was the responsibility of the Scottish Office, and its approaches did not mirror those in England. Until 1979, a general consent for council house sales had only operated in Scotland between 1972 and 1974 (Scottish Development Department, 1972, 1974). This does not mean that the Scottish Office did not approve individual cases, and its capacity to assess these was arguably greater than in England. Between 1970 and 1973, 62 Scottish councils sold a total of 892 council dwellings; only 19 councils had sold 10 or more dwellings, and 31% of all sales had been in Edinburgh. The general consent generated 6,972 sales between 1973 and 1979.

The Housing Tenants' Rights Etc Act (Scotland) 1980 enacted the same Right to Buy proposals as England and Wales, but following devolution, in 1998 the Scottish Parliament and government made changes because of the pressures that the Right to Buy was placing on the social housing sector (Jones and Murie, 2006, pp 42-46). The Housing (Scotland) Act 2001 did not alter arrangements for existing tenants who retained a Preserved Right to Buy with a qualifying period of two years and discounts of 60% for houses and 70% for flats. For new or transferring tenants (taking up a tenancy after 30 September 2002) introduced a 'Modernised' Right to Buy with less generous discounts (starting at 20% after 5 years and rising by 1% for every additional year of tenancy to a maximum of 35% after 20 years and with a cash maximum of £15,000). The Modernised Right to Buy would also apply to most housing association tenants after 10 years, although housing associations could apply to the Scottish government to extend this period.

The 'Modernised' Right to Buy introduced a common set of rights, within a single standard secure tenancy for all social sector tenants, introduced at the same time. Tenants who already had the Right to Buy had their existing rights ring-fenced, and the longer qualifying period and lower discounts (with the same rates for flats and houses) only applied to new tenants. The Housing (Scotland) Act 2001 also introduced a procedure for the identification and designation of pressured areas where the Right to Buy would be suspended, to safeguard the continued availability of social rented housing. The thinking behind these changes was that the Right to Buy had been operating in isolation or possibly at variance with other policies. Compared with other policies (including cash incentives for tenants to move elsewhere to buy), the Right to Buy was expensive and it could cause problems in some areas. The conclusion was that it should be 'rebalanced rather than removed', to meet the aspirations of low-income households and the objectives of communities (Jones and Murie, 2006).

The Housing (Scotland) Act 2010 transferred powers related to pressured area designations from the Scottish government to local authorities (from 30 June 2011), provided that particular housing types could be designated as pressured, and increased the maximum period for designation from five to ten years. The arrangements for pressured areas became less important, however, as the Scottish government took steps leading to the abolition of the Right to Buy. Legislation in 2010 ended (from 1 March 2011) the Right to Buy for houses built or acquired after 15 June 2008, and ended the Right to Buy for first-time tenants in the social housing sector (whose tenancies began on, or after, 2 March 2011). Following a consultation process in 2012, Deputy First Minister Nicola Sturgeon announced (July 2013) the intention to end the Right to Buy, to protect social houses from sale:

> We can no longer afford to see badly needed homes lost to the social sector. That is why I am today announcing the final stage of the abolition of the Right to Buy – a decision that will safeguard Scotland's social housing stock for the benefit of citizens today and for our future generations. (quoted in Parkin, 2015)

The abolition of the Right to Buy would mean that dwellings that would otherwise have been sold (initially estimated at more than 25,000 dwellings over five years, revised to more than 15,500), would remain in the social rented sector and be available for rent over their lifetime. This would increase housing supply and choice, reduce waiting lists, protect the asset base of social landlords and assist their forward planning. By not being marginalised, social housing would play a vital role in building sustainable mixed communities. Although the abolition of Right to Buy would be detrimental for qualifying tenants, there were other schemes to support tenants to become homeowners. Part 1 of the Housing (Scotland) Act 2014 abolished the Right to Buy. Social housing tenants who had the Right to Buy had until 31 July 2016 to exercise it, with detailed provisions applying to tenants with Preserved Right to Buy, Modernised Right to Buy, and where pressured area designation applied.

Wales

Restrictions on the Right to Buy in Wales were initially similar to those in England and involved reduction in the maximum discount (from £24,000 to £16,000) in 2003. The Housing (Wales) Measure 2011, however, introduced a procedure similar to that for Scotland under which local authorities could apply for suspension of the Right to Buy in areas where there was high pressure on housing – where demand for social housing substantially exceeds its supply or is likely to do so, and the imbalance between supply and demand is likely to increase as a result of the exercise of the Right to Buy and related rights. This suspension would be for a period of up to five years, although local authorities could apply to extend this, and could apply to all social housing in a local authority area, to all social housing in certain parts of an area, or to certain types of social housing.

The Welsh government introduced new proposals on the Right to Buy following a consultation on the future of the Right to Buy and Right to Acquire (Welsh Government, 2015), that ended in April 2015. This consultation resulted in 63% of respondents – including councils, housing associations and social housing tenants – favouring developing legislation to end the Right to Buy in Wales. Following this, a White Paper put forward two proposals, aimed at protecting the existing social housing stock from further reduction, for public consultation. These would involve either changing existing legislation to reduce the maximum discount from £16,000 to £8,000 for tenants applying to buy their home from their council or housing association, or developing new legislation that would end the Right to Buy and Right to Acquire. The Welsh government explained that the proposed changes to the Right to Buy were intended to protect social housing stock:

> Over the last thirty years or so, the Right to Buy and Right to Acquire have allowed many tenants in social housing to buy their home from their Local Authority or Housing Association. As a result, there has been a significant reduction in our social housing stock....
>
> In the current financial climate, for housing, economic and other factors have combined to cause considerable pressure on the supply of homes. The pressures affect many but the effect on people whose needs cannot be met by the housing market is particularly noticeable. Some people cannot afford to buy a home, or to rent a home from a private landlord. They are dependent on social housing or some other form of subsidised provision. Social housing is a particularly important safety net. (quoted in Parkin, 2015)

On 3 June 2015, the Minister for Communities and Tackling Poverty, Lesley Griffiths, announced that, after considering the consultation responses, she had decided to proceed with both proposals. A Statutory Instrument reduced the maximum discount from £16,000 to £8,000 from 14 July 2015, and new primary legislation would end the Right to Buy. She stated:

> Social housing is a vital and very valuable part of our housing system and is an essential safety net for people for whom the housing market does not work, either by buying a property or by renting from a private landlord. Significantly, this includes some of the most vulnerable people in our communities. (quoted in Parkin, 2015)

While the responses to the consultation indicated some support for reducing the maximum discount to an even lower figure, the reduction to £8,000 was thought to be reasonable and proportionate in terms of the desire to stem the continued reduction in social housing. The new legislation to end the Right to Buy and the Right to Acquire was regarded as ultimately the only way to protect the social housing stock from further reduction and, most importantly, to ensure as many people as possible have access to a home they can afford (Welsh Government, 2015).

Northern Ireland

The Government of Ireland Act 1920 established a distinctive system for the government of Northern Ireland, with housing one of the matters devolved to an elected Parliament. Until this was suspended, Northern Ireland pursued a separate housing policy, and there were major legislative differences and variations in investment in public housing. Unlike some other devolved policy areas, there was little attempt to achieve parity in housing policy with the rest of the UK, and controversies over housing matters contributed to social and political conflicts and the decision to suspend the Stormont Parliament in 1972 (Birrell and Murie, 1980). Some 155,000 public sector dwellings were brought together under the ownership and control of the Northern

Ireland Housing Executive (NIHE) established in 1972 prior to any extensive sales programme. In view of the importance of housing in political conflicts in Northern Ireland, Westminster governments consistently maintained higher levels of investment in housing than elsewhere in the UK. Consequently, the poorest quality properties and most of the multi-storey properties in the Housing Executive stock were demolished, a higher proportion of the stock has been built since 1970, and standards of maintenance, repair and management have been at a consistently higher level than elsewhere in the UK.

The NIHE adopted a house sales scheme for the first time in 1973, and some 2,246 sales were completed between 1973 and 1979. The legislation introducing the Right to Buy in 1980 did not apply to Northern Ireland, but the NIHE revised its voluntary policy in 1979 to operate broadly in line with the Right to Buy, with some detailed differences notably enabling all tenants to apply to buy their home with no minimum tenancy qualification. The Housing (NI) Order 1983 formally adopted the Right to Buy. Tenants of less than two years' standing were entitled to buy under the house sales scheme at 30% discount. Those with two years' tenancy were entitled to a discount of 32%, and this was increased by 1% for each additional year up to a maximum of 50%. Arrangements related to historic costs (referring to capital investment since September 1973), and resale within five years (where there was provision for discount to be repaid on a pro rata basis), were essentially the same as elsewhere in the UK.

Significantly the NIHE was subject to a more generous regime with respect to the use of capital receipts generated by its sales. Until this was effectively terminated in 2000, attitudes to sales in Northern Ireland were positive because of the capacity to reinvest proceeds from sales. After 1979, adjustments to the NIHE sales scheme were broadly in line with those of the Right to Buy in England: maximum discounts were increased to 60% in 1984 and differential discounts were introduced between houses and flats in 1986. The basis for calculating historic cost was changed in 1989 to an eight-year rolling calculation, and the repayment of discount period was reduced from five to three years in 1986. In Northern Ireland after 1996 there was an important policy shift with responsibility for building new social housing transferred from the Housing Executive to housing associations. This was made conditional on housing associations making it known on what terms, if at all, they would be prepared to sell the homes, and the largest housing associations in Northern Ireland operated a Voluntary Purchase Grant scheme. However, the number of sales carried out by housing associations was low, rising from 25 in 1996/97 to 78 in 1999/2000, after which both NIHE and housing association tenants were subject to the same scheme (Atkinson and Goodlad, 2002).

Northern Ireland had generally followed the rest of the UK in its approach to selling public sector housing, but when concerns over the loss of social rented housing and about value for money began to affect attitudes to discounts elsewhere, Northern Ireland was reluctant to follow: reduced maximum discounts in the rest of the UK after 1998 were not adopted immediately. A maximum discount of £34,000 was introduced in 2002 and in 2004, following consultation, the policy brought more into line with the rest of the UK, with the maximum discount reduced to £24,000, the qualifying period for eligibility to buy increased from two to five years, and the period for which historic costs were taken into account increased from eight to ten years. Perhaps more significantly, the discount formula started at a lower level (20% after five years), but advanced more rapidly (by 2% for each additional year up to a maximum of 60%), and the policy was extended to the very small housing association sector. Tenants could also buy a share in the property (paying rent on the remaining portion). Some properties were excluded from the scheme, including sheltered dwellings and a single-storey or ground-floor dwellings (other than a flat) with no more than two bedrooms.

Conclusions

The Right to Buy grew out of earlier discretionary schemes and electoral promises made over a period exceeding 10 years. It involved three significant breaches with the past. First, it removed local discretion and introduced a common approach irrespective of local housing situations and local politics. Second, it introduced much more substantial discounts than had applied previously with no real justification for these. Third, the policy package of which it formed part involved reduced investment in council housing, rising rents and a shift away from a managed to a market approach, with universal housing benefits replacing bricks and mortar subsidies.

Over the 35 years since 1980 there were important changes in the Right to Buy, and three phases of policy are apparent:

- The first phase (1980-86) operated with the arrangements set up in 1980 and with some detailed amendments in 1984. Although housing public expenditure had been severely cut, there was still a small council housebuilding programme at this stage.
- The second phase (1986-98) involved a significant break with earlier arrangements and higher, differential rates of discount for flats. Sales prices barely related to market values, and households could qualify for enormous discounts after a few years as a tenant. The Right to Buy was now seen, along with stock transfer, as part of a policy to dismantle council housing. There was very little investment in new council housing and active promotion of housing associations as a private sector alternative protected from the Right to Buy.
- In the third phase (1998-2016) divergent approaches emerged between the UK nations. Concerns about value for money and the effect of the Right to Buy led to reductions in maximum discounts across the UK, but subsequently Scotland and Wales moved towards abolition of the Right to Buy while the policy was revitalised in England.

In Scotland and Wales, the overriding reason for the restriction (and then abolition) of the Right to Buy was that, with the low rate of new additions, it was desirable to protect the supply of social housing from sale. In England there were also low rates of new additions to social housing, but neither the coalition government nor commentators urging extension of the Right to Buy paid attention to the accumulated evidence about it, or the arguments being advanced in other parts of the UK. There was no engagement with alternative views that were dismissed or ignored.

Housing associations had largely escaped the Right to Buy, but other policies provided opportunities for their tenants to become homeowners. In Scotland, Wales and Northern Ireland additional measures had extended Right to Buy policies to some or all housing association tenants, but because general approaches to the sale of public housing in these parts of the UK had become more measured, this meant extending less generous schemes – with longer qualifying periods and lower discounts than applied in England.

Stock transfers had served to protect a significant part of the social rented sector (especially in England) from the Right to Buy, and the development of private financing made the expansion of social renting outside the reach of the Right to Buy attractive to governments, especially when they were concerned about the supply of affordable housing. But, especially at election times, issues of supply and value for money were not always paramount, and electoral appeal and short-term financial flows made the Right to Buy attractive. More fundamentally, it is not clear that the concerns expressed repeatedly in the 60 years before 1979, over the price at which public assets were sold, had much effect on policy decisions. Discounts were extraordinary in 1980 and became more so through the period to 1998, and the approach to selling co-ownership dwellings appears to have been unconcerned with achieving a return for the public purse. This approach was modified to some extent across the UK after 1998, and more fundamental changes were introduced in Scotland and Wales. But the increased discounts in England, after 2010, suggest that dismantling public and collective provision had become an end in itself rather than a means to expanding home ownership. There had been no consultation on extending or restricting the Right to Buy in England in the lead-up to the 2015 general election. New proposals related to the Right to Buy emerged, as it had done in the past, as part of a Conservative electoral strategy rather than a housing strategy.

4
STATISTICS AND IMPACTS OF THE RIGHT TO BUY

Introduction

This chapter draws on available statistics to indicate activity under the Right to Buy and its impact. More than 2.8 million council and social rented dwellings were sold in the UK under the Right to Buy between 1980 and 2015, generating more than £58 billion in capital receipts for government. The Right to Buy changed the size, nature and location of public and social rented housing across the UK, and contributed to a significant change in the overall tenure structure.

The government has provided statistics on council house sales since before 1980, but there are problems over changing definitions and practices. Some data are for financial and some for calendar years. Some refer to a narrow definition of sales carried out under the Right to Buy, and others to all sales to sitting tenants. Regional data for England ceased to be compiled after 2011. Local variations in rates of sale are difficult to present for local authorities that transferred any significant part of their stock. Consequently, this chapter does not provide a comprehensive or definitive statistical account, and aims to provide sufficient statistics to present a reliable picture that highlights key aspects of the Right to Buy.

Sales of public and social housing, 1980-2015

Table 4.1 presents data for the annual sales of dwellings in England, Scotland, Wales and Northern Ireland by councils, new towns and housing associations. These data refer to Right to Buy Sales and its equivalent in Northern Ireland, and exclude other sales of existing social housing. They indicate almost 2.7 million sales in the UK between 1980 and 2015. It may be argued that some sales usually recorded as 'other sales to sitting tenants' should be added to these figures. These were highest in England and Wales in 1979 and 1980 and the years immediately following, with some 40,000 such sales in 1979 and a further 128,200 between the beginning of 1980 and end of 1986 (Forrest and Murie, 1988, pp 112-13). A further 31,783 other sales to sitting tenants are referred to between 1991 and 2014/15. If these figures are included, the total sales achieved under the Right to Buy in the UK between 1979 and 2015 were over 2.85 million.

Table 4.1: All Right to Buy Sales (local authorities, new towns and housing associations), 1980-2015

	England	Scotland	Wales	Great Britain	Northern Ireland	Total UK
1980	55	2,157	0	2,212	473	2,685
1981	66,321	10,096	7,916	84,333	6,504	90,837
1982	174,697	13,544	16,088	204,329	6,199	210,528
1983	120,659	17,321	9,228	147,208	5,367	152,575
1984	86,315	15,248	5,650	107,213	5,665	112,878
1985	78,433	14,273	5,622	98,328	4,330	102,658
1986	77,114	13,322	5,420	95,856	3,660	99,516
1987	86,845	18,594	5,609	111,048	2,802	113,850
1988	132,980	31,480	9,605	174,065	3,000	177,065
1989	144,754	38,443	12,753	195,950	4,340	200,290
1990	96,729	32,535	6,487	135,751	4,474	140,225
1991	53,462	22,694	3,503	79,659	3,290	82,949
1992	42,280	23,521	2,823	68,624	3,234	71,858
1993	42,034	19,787	2,814	64,635	3,710	68,345
1994	45,875	21,125	3,132	70,132	4,693	74,825
1995	34,553	16,500	2,369	53,422	4,765	58,187
1996	35,583	13,023	2,093	50,699	4,665	55,364

	England	Scotland	Wales	Great Britain	Northern Ireland	Total UK
1997	45,829	17,369	2,632	65,830	4,907	70,737
1998	44,686	14,948	2,614	62,248	4,395	66,643
1999	61,496	14,227	3,466	79,189	4,526	83,715
2000	59,478	14,935	3,522	77,935	5,555	83,490
2001	60,192	14,095	3,446	77,733	5,011	82,744
2002	73,867	17,343	4,288	95,498	5,991	101,489
2003	84,102	20,698	6,924	111,724	5,652	117,376
2004	58,648	15,203	5,064	78,915	3,135	82,050
2005	33,010	13,033	2,084	48,127	2,522	50,649
2006	22,519	10,471	1,367	34,357	2,201	36,558
2007	17,684	8,790	1,017	25,000	800	25,800
2008	12,043	4,041	331	8,237	54	8,291
2009	2,869	2,178	110	5,467	272	5,739
2010	2,375	2,024	182	5,920	250	6,170
2011	2,758	1,584	171	5,499	250	5,749
2012	2,638	1,372	170	9,944	290	10,234
2013	5,944	1,292	253	17,227	549	17,776
2014	11,261				470	
2015	12,304					
Total	1,916,294	497,405	138,753	2,552,452	118,001	2,669,845

Source: Wilcox (various years) Housing finance review and Housing review; Forrest and Murie (1990a)

Many more sales were completed under the Right to Buy than were anticipated by some commentators in 1980. Some local authorities and others (House of Commons, 1981) assumed that take-up of the Right to Buy would be low because the income and occupational characteristics of tenants severely limited the numbers able to buy. In practice, there was an immediate substantial impact through discretionary sales, before Right to Buy became law, but under the same framework with the same discounts as for the Right to Buy. This, and the rapid build-up of Right to Buy sales after 1980, suggests that there was pent-up demand. The levels of discount at this stage were above the 20% maximum that had generally applied before 1979. It is not clear whether these higher levels of discount were necessary to achieve sales from established tenants committed to their existing homes. Questions remain over whether a similar volume of sales would have been achieved without such high discounts. Subsequent changes in discounts appear to have affected the volume of sales, but may have represented unnecessarily high rewards, and also encouraged abuses that persuaded some tenants to buy on a more speculative basis.

Figure 4.1 charts the annual fluctuation of Right to Buy sales. The surge in sales following the introduction of the Right to Buy in 1980 is generally associated with both pent-up demand from areas where discretionary sales had not operated, and with new demand generated by more generous terms for sale and the publicity associated with new legislation. The pattern of fluctuation was similar in England, Scotland and Wales. Sales peaked initially in 1981 in Northern Ireland, in 1982 in England and Wales, and in 1983 in Scotland. After this they declined in each case, before increasing sharply again in an improved economic and housing market climate and affected by higher discounts. The second peak was reached in 1990 in Northern Ireland and 1989 elsewhere. The second surge of sales was more marked in Scotland and in the Northern regions of England, and there was some levelling up of regional differences.

Changes in policy and prices for purchase appear to have had a significant impact, but employment, incomes and confidence in the economy are important in the explanation of trends (Foulis, 1985, 1987; Murie and Wang, 1992). In Scotland, the second peak, in 1989, involved more than twice the level of sales than in 1983, and meant a narrowing of the gap in tenure structures between Scotland and the rest of the UK. Although policy changes and contextual factors explain part of the fluctuation in rates of sale, changing employment or household circumstances enabled households that had previously been unable or unwilling to buy to purchase. The gap between rents and mortgage payments on discounted purchases was often small and within a short period, non-existent. The Right to Buy enabled households that liked the home they lived in to buy it and change the pattern of payments for it: rather than paying rent (probably rising in real terms) for the rest of their lives, purchasing generally meant diminishing and ultimately no payments for house purchase.

Figure 4.1: Right to Buy sales, England, Scotland, Wales and Great Britain, 1980-2013

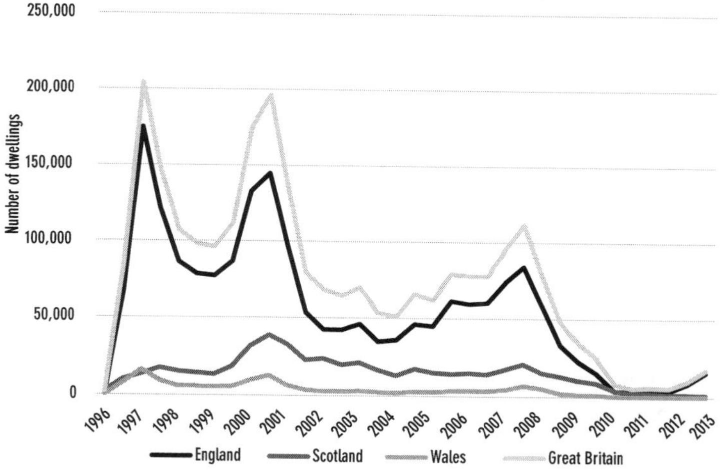

Source: Table 4.1

A third peak in sales in 2003 in England, Scotland and Wales and 2002 in Northern Ireland attested to the continuing appeal of the Right to Buy. The third peak was lower in terms of numbers but almost as high as the previous peaks as a proportion of the stock available for sale. Higher sales at this stage were associated with changed economic conditions and housing market trends. Rising employment, increased affluence and a booming homeownership market attracted more people to buy properties. The reduced discounts in England in 1999 did not evidently deter purchasers, but the further reductions in 2003 (and the reductions in Northern Ireland in 2004) appear to have done so. Suggestions that the Right to Buy was about to be revoked or made less accessible had also encouraged some people to bring forward plans to buy.

Right to Buy sales had declined to very low levels by the time of the global financial crisis from 2007/08 onwards, when consequent problems in accessing mortgage loans, the collapse of transactions and fall in house prices further undermined the attraction of the Right to Buy. In England the lowest level of annual sales since the Right to Buy was introduced was recorded in 2005, and again in each successive year until 2009. As the decline had commenced before the credit crunch and the economic crisis that it triggered, these factors are not sufficient to explain the initial fall in Right to Buy sales or its duration. In England Right to Buy sales increased slightly after 2010, before the reintroduction of higher discounts by the coalition government in 2012 (and 2013 for London). The changes in Scotland and Wales also appear to have prevented any recovery in sales associated with a weakening of the impact of the economic crisis.

It might be concluded that, in addition to policy changes and economic and housing market factors, the fact that a much smaller stock was available to be bought under the Right to Buy, and that what remained was less attractive, had a continuing impact. The explanation for low sales also relates to uncertainties about future incomes and the economy and access to mortgages, especially for lower-income households and those in insecure employment. In Scotland and Wales Right to Buy sales remained low after 2010, even after the worst effects of economic recession were over. The different trajectories of Scotland (and to a lesser extent Wales) and England and Northern Ireland are partly explained by policy differences.

Properties and places

The properties sold under the Right to Buy and earlier sales under discretionary powers did not represent a cross-section of dwelling types, and there were continuing variations in rates of sale in different places. They were disproportionately more attractive, better quality and larger houses with gardens and houses rather than flats (Forrest and Murie, 1984a, 1984b, 1990b; Foulis, 1985, 1987; Kerr, 1988). In England more than half of sitting tenant purchasers bought semi-detached houses, although only a third of public sector tenants lived in such dwellings; only 3% of purchasers bought apartments, but almost a third of tenants lived in such dwellings. There were fewer sales of acquired properties, of properties in less popular estates and of small dwellings. Holmans (1993) suggested that by 1991, 44% of semi-detached family houses had been sold in England compared with 18% of the smaller terraced houses and only 7% of flats.

Sales of flats increased after the higher discounts for flats were introduced in 1986. While flats remained heavily under-represented in the overall total of sales, by the 1990s they accounted for over a quarter of all annual disposals in England. This pattern of sales has considerably changed the profile of the council housing stock in England. The proportion of public sector tenants living in flats increased significantly between 1981 and 1993. Households on the waiting list for council housing were much more likely to be offered a flat than in the past, and the contrast between home ownership and council housing became more pronounced in terms of dwelling type.

The changing pattern is illustrated by Birmingham, where council housing became more concentrated in certain parts of the city. The early progress of council house sales generated a zonal pattern, with most sales in a middle ring and fewer sales in the inner city and peripheral estates, but the longer-term pattern is more one of a patchwork, with differences related to property type, construction date and estate reputation. Within this patchwork, however, a greater proportion of dwellings were sold in the more popular, leafy, suburban council estates of houses and gardens and of traditional construction.

Table 4.2 shows the shifting importance of flats among all Right to Buy sales in England. Tenants of flats were initially less likely to buy their properties, but higher discounts for flats and maisonettes had an impact on the rate of sales. From a low initial level there was a significant increase in the proportion of flat sales in 1988 and later, but the proportion of flat sales was sustained at a high level through the 2000s.

Table 4.2: Flat sales as a proportion of social housing sales in England, 1980-2014

	Right to Buy sales of flats (%)		
Year	**Local authority**	**Housing associations**	**All social housing**
1980			
1981	2		
1982	2.8		
1983	6.6		
1984	5.7		
1985	7.6		
1986	9.0		
1987	10.0		
1986-87	7%	n/a	n/a
1987-88	11%	n/a	n/a
1988-89	17%	n/a	n/a
1989-90	19%	n/a	n/a
1990-91	23%	n/a	n/a
1991-92	24%	n/a	n/a
1992-93	18%	n/a	n/a
1993-94	14%	n/a	n/a
1994-95	11%	n/a	n/a
1995-96	11%	n/a	n/a
1996-97	12%	10%	**12%**
1997-98	12%	10%	**12%**
1998-99	14%	12%	**14%**
1999-00	14%	11%	**14%**
2000-01	20%	11%	**19%**
2001-02	20%	11%	**19%**
2002-03	22%	14%	**21%**
2003-04	22%	11%	**20%**
2004-05	28%	11%	**25%**
2005-06	26%	12%	**23%**
2006-07	25%	12%	**22%**
2007-08	27%	13%	**23%**
2008-09	31%	14%	**27%**
2009-10	22%	13%	**19%**
2010-11	26%	15%	**23%**
2011-12	26%	12%	**22%**
2012-13	27%	8%	**21%**
2013-14	32%	13%	**26%**
2014-15	37%	17%	**34%**

Sources: Annual figures in italics from Department of the Environment housing and construction statistics, quoted in Jones and Murie (2006, p 57). Other statistics are from DCLG Live tables, Social housing sales, Table 681

In Scotland, sales of flats had always been proportionately higher than in England, arising from their greater significance in the public sector stock. However, a similarly dramatic increase was apparent (see Figure 4.2), with flat sales accounting for around one in ten sales in the early 1980s and four in ten by 1990. Sales of flats in Scotland continued at a relatively high level, and out of 494,590 Right to Buy sales in Scotland between 1980 and 2015, 154,691 (31%) were flats.

Figure 4.2: Public sector house sales in Scotland:1979-2015

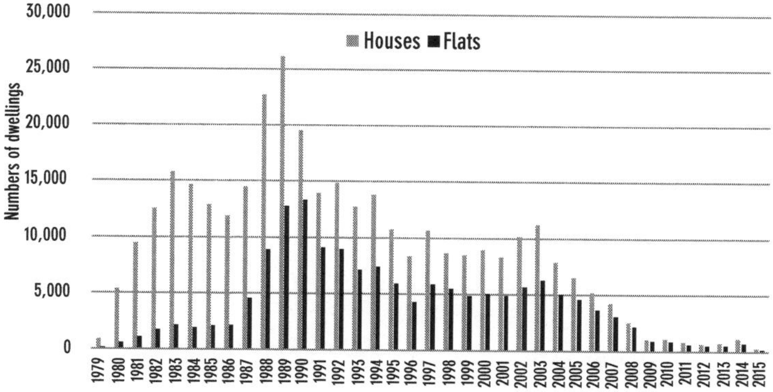

Source: Scottish Government Live Tables/sales to sitting tenants

In Northern Ireland between 1979 and 1992 only 3% of sold dwellings were flats and maisonettes, although these properties accounted for a fifth of stock in 1992 (NIHE, 1992). Sales were concentrated in postwar, pre-1971 terraced houses, in provincial towns and rural locations.

The rate of sales completed varied within as well as between the different countries of the UK. In England in the early years of the Right to Buy the Northern regions lagged behind, and the South East, East and South West had the highest rates of sale (see Table 4.3). The Northern regions of England show a pattern more like that of Scotland than of the Southern regions of England in the early 1980s. However, they did not follow the Scottish surge of sales in the late 1980s.

Table 4.3: Stock and sales in the English regions

	Council stock, December 1979		All sales, 1979-87		All sales, 1980/81 to 2010/11	
	000s	% of England	No	% of England	No	% of England
North East	489	9	65,249	8	156,180	9
North West	751	14	94,728	12	211,690	12
Yorkshire and the Humber	617	12	70,393	9	205,070	12
East Midlands	425	8	76,313	9	163,160	9
West Midlands	647	12	95,347	12	216,120	12
East	192	4	36,977	5	185,340	10
London	853	16	113,455	14	290,820	16
South East	914	17	193,752	24	204,710	12
South West	369	7	68,134	8	139,330	8
England	5,257	100	814,358	100	1,772,240	100

Source: Forrest and Murie (1988); and DCLG, Table 670

Regional statistics ceased to be made available for the years after 2010/11, and the rates of Right to Buy sales recorded until then are increasingly difficult to interpret because of stock transfers. The high numbers of transfers in the South East had a sharp impact on Right to Buy sales in later years. Leaving this aside, it is likely that regional differences became less marked through the whole Right to Buy period. This seems less likely to be true for local differences, but analysis at a local level is increasingly difficult because of stock transfers. Some early explanations for major variations in rates of sale between local authorities, including those that were attractive to the government, emphasised the reluctance of local authorities to sell and to administrative and political delays. The actions taken by central government to minimise mean that, beyond the first year of Right to Buy sales, variations in sales are not attributable to this. As with the regional figures, the evidence suggests that differences in economic circumstances, the nature of council housing within the area, the relative attractiveness of council housing compared with other tenures, price and dwelling-type factors, local housing market conditions and price levels, all affected rates of sale (Dunn et al, 1987; Forrest and Murie, 1988). The highest rates of sale were in two belts, one across the South and one across the North of England. There were also some strong rates of sale in shire districts in all regions except for Yorkshire and Humberside. The lowest belt of sales was associated with the cross-Pennine route from the Mersey to the Humber and north of that, and there are relatively low rates of sales in the West Midlands conurbation and Tyneside.

By the end of 2001-02, 20 local authorities in England had sold less than 20% of their stock and 39 had sold 40%. Variation within regions was greater than that between them. No authority in Yorkshire and Humberside (and only one each in the West Midlands and North East) had sold 40% or more of its stock. The variation in the rate of sales was greatest in London and the South East of England. In London, six boroughs recorded less than 20% of their stock sold, 20 less than 30% and 13 (including the City of London) over 30%. In the South East outside London three districts recorded less than 20% of their stock sold, 19 less than 30% and 48 more than 30%. The impact of the Right to Buy has been to increase the relative concentration of rented housing in London and to increase the contrast between the tenure structure in London and in the South East.

In the early years of the Right to Buy the highest selling local authorities in England were smaller rural and shire district councils and the lowest selling authorities were large urban authorities, in particular, in inner London and the North West of England (Forrest and Murie, 1984a, 1984b, 1988, 1990a). This variation remained as sales volumes increased. Right to Buy sales were highest in areas where owner-occupation was already at high levels. There were also strong rates of sale in new towns and in shire districts in all regions except for Yorkshire and Humberside. In the North of England Right to Buy sales lagged behind sales in the more prosperous South East and South West, but these differences then levelled off (Jones and Murie, 2006). As in England, there was a significant variation in sales at a local level within Scotland, Wales and Northern Ireland. By the end of 1995, the highest rates of sale in Scotland were in the five new towns, Scottish Homes and in Badenoch and Strathspey (49%), North-East Fife (43%) and Stewartry (41%). The lowest rates of sale were in Glasgow (17%), Inverclyde (18%) and Motherwell (20%). In Wales the highest rates of sale were in Taff-Ely (46%) and Port Talbot (45%), and the lowest rate of sale was in Rhondda (17%), followed by Swansea (25%). In Northern Ireland there were considerable variations in the rates of sale at district level within the NIHE, with the highest rates of sales in the South region and the lowest in Belfast (20%).

The overall picture is that better properties in better locations (within and between districts) were more likely to be sold. This was associated with dwelling characteristics and locations and also household characteristics (with poorer and more recent tenants more likely to live in less attractive properties). This was consistent with the evidence of what had happened under previous discretionary policies, although these had lower discounts (before 1979), and generally only included council built houses.

Discounts, property values and capital receipts

Discussions of the Right to Buy and its impact refer to the level of discounts and of capital receipts. Discounts have represented both incentives to purchase and expenditures or income foregone by government. Key issues relate to whether the levels of discount have been appropriate or excessive, and this refers to considerations of whether the government could have achieved broadly the same result for less, and whether discounts have been fair (between different households that have benefited to different extents, and between households able to benefit and those not qualifying), and whether they have been proportionate.

Changes in discount arrangements as well as in property values affected the progress of the Right to Buy and the levels of capital receipts generated by it. The average discount on sales of properties in England had risen to 50% by 1983-85, and rose further to a peak of 52% in 1990–91, when the proportion of flats among sold property was relatively high. Discounts fell as a percentage of value from 50% in 1998/99 to 24% in 2007/08 as rising property values meant that more purchases were affected by maximum discount arrangements. Maximum discounts were less generous, but this halted the growth in the cash value of discounts rather than reduced it (see Table 4.4). These data suggest that higher levels of maximum discount were not necessary to generate sales, and changes in discount arrangements after 1998 did not reduce the cash value of discounts. The increase in maximum discounts associated with the relaunch of the Right to Buy

Table 4.4: Local authority sales in England, 1998-2015: financial details

	Local authority sales				
	Sales	Average capital receipts per dwelling (£)	Average discount per dwelling (£)	Average market value per dwelling (£)	**Discount as % of market value**
1998-99	40,272	22,610	22,880	45,490	50
1999-2000	54,251	25,320	23,630	48,950	48
2000-01	52,380	27,220	23,880	51,090	47
2001-02	51,968	30,140	23,380	53,520	44
2002-03	63,394	34,860	23,790	58,660	41
2003-04	69,577	42,200	24,640	66,840	37
2004-05	49,983	51,520	25,650	77,180	33
2005-06	26,654	57,950	25,530	83,480	31
2006-07	17,684	67,800	24,970	92,770	27
2007-08	12,043	78,130	25,340	103,470	24
2008-09	2,869	76,850	25,400	102,250	25
2009-10	2,375	75,200	26,580	101,780	26
2010-11	2,758	77,470	26,510	103,970	25
2011-12	2,638	73,350	26,690	100,040	27
2012-13	5,944	63,040	51,760	114,800	45
2013-14	11,261	68,820	60,300	129,120	47
2014-15	12,304	76,380	65,140	141,520	46

Source: DCLG Live tables, Social housing sales, Table 682

after 2011 generated considerably higher rates of discount. Average discounts rose after 2012 and, although average sale prices were higher, average capital receipts were lower than previously.

A smaller number of sales were completed in England by housing associations, but Table 4.5 indicates that discounts represented a higher proportion of market value.

Table 4.5: Right to Buy sales by housing associations in England, 1988-2015

	Registered provider social housing sales				
	Sales	Average capital receipts per dwelling (£)	Average discount per dwelling (£)	Average market value per dwelling (£)	**Discount as % of market value**
1998-99	4,414	24,830	25,980	51,460	**50**
1999-2000	7,245	27,060	25,970	53,220	**49**
2000-01	7,098	27,400	24,860	52,520	**47**
2001-02	8,224	26,690	23,600	50,780	**46**
2002-03	10,473	32,500	26,300	59,370	**44**
2003-04	14,525	33,200	25,420	58,640	**43**
2004-05	8,665	37,600	26,590	64,210	**41**
2005-06	6,356	45,010	27,150	72,160	**38**
2006-07	4,835	53,460	28,390	81,960	**35**
2007-08	3,150	62,630	27,120	89,750	**30**
2008-09	996	72,230	26,940	99,170	**27**
2009-10	804	62,720	28,010	91,530	**31**
2010-11	956	64,860	28,130	95,330	**30**
2011-12	1,106	61,140	28,410	90,380	**31**
2012-13	2,458	49,510	50,120	100,460	**50**
2013-14	4,421	51,060	54,240	105,300	**52**
2014-15	4,215	51,060	54,920	105,980	52

Source: DCLG Live Tables, Social housing sales, Table 682

Figure 4.3 presents data for the regions of England on changes in the market value of properties sold under the RTB. In the regions of the North and Midlands there were limited increases in market values through the 1980s and 1990s, with a much steeper increase in the early 2000s until values stagnated or fell after 2007. The pattern for the Southern regions (London, South East, East, South West) was more dramatic with a greater increase in values throughout the period until a collapse in 2007. These trends affect confidence and the appeal of purchase and affordability.

Against this background, Figure 4.4, referring to the regional average cash value of discounts, provides a different perspective. The cash value of discounts generally increased until the mid-1990s, but rising property values meant that discount limits began to affect more sales. The cash value of discounts did not generally decline as a result but these represented a smaller percentage of market value – some 50% in 1998 and 25% in 2010/11. London was, however affected at an

Figure 4.3: Estimated average market values of dwellings sold under the Right to Buy by local authorities in England: Regions 1998/9 to 2010/11

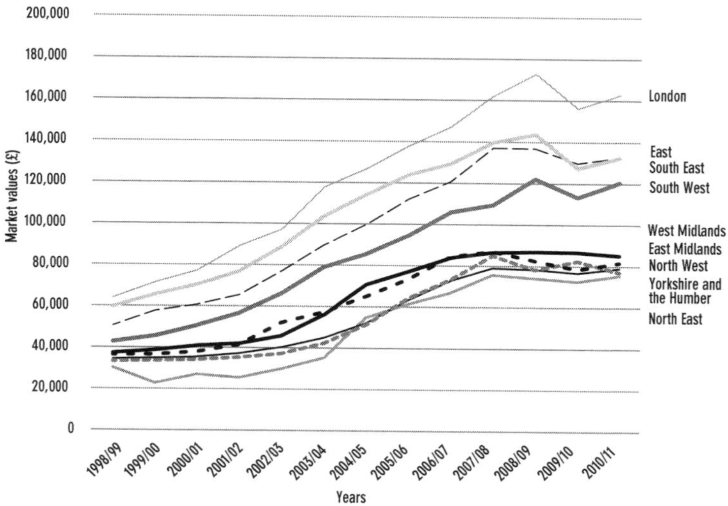

Source: DCLG Live Tables, Table 643

earlier stage and changes in discounts after 1998 had more impact on the Southern regions and a dramatic effect on London.

In Northern Ireland average discounts were slightly lower than in England (46% in 1986 and 48% in the subsequent period to 1992), perhaps reflecting the lower proportion of flats in the stock and among sales (NIHE, 1992).

Figure 4.4: Estimated average value of discount for dwellings sold under the Right to Buy by local authorities in England: Regions 1998/9 – 2010/11

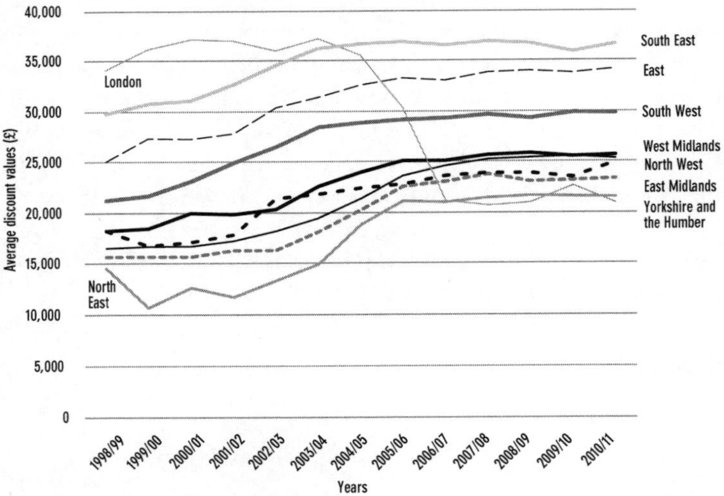

Source: DCLG Live Tables, Table 643

It is important to recognise that housing market changes as well as policy differences have had an impact on the operation of the Right to Buy. Confidence in the continuation of rising house prices affected take-up of the Right to Buy, but if prices became too high, that could affect affordability; and if prices stagnated, potential purchasers appeared to become less confident about buying. In Scotland, for example, the years between 1980 and 2002/03 saw a slow increase in average market values, but these then doubled from 2002/03 to

2008/09. Average market value peaked in 2008/9 and remained below that through to 2015 (see Figure 4.5).

In every year between 1998/99 and 2002/03, the value of Right to Buy discounts was considerably more than expenditure by the government on the Affordable Housing programme. For example, in 2002/03 the value of Right to Buy discounts was £1.5 billion, compared with £0.9 billion invested in the Affordable Housing programme.

Before 1980, building societies were cautious about lending to fund Right to Buy purchases. In the event, however, high discounts made the risks associated with private sector lending to Right to Buy purchasers very low, and this increased the willingness of building societies to finance Right to Buy purchases. In addition, both the

Figure 4.5: Scotland: average value of all sales of public housing (Rent to Mortgage, Right to Buy, voluntary sales), 1996/97 to 2014/15

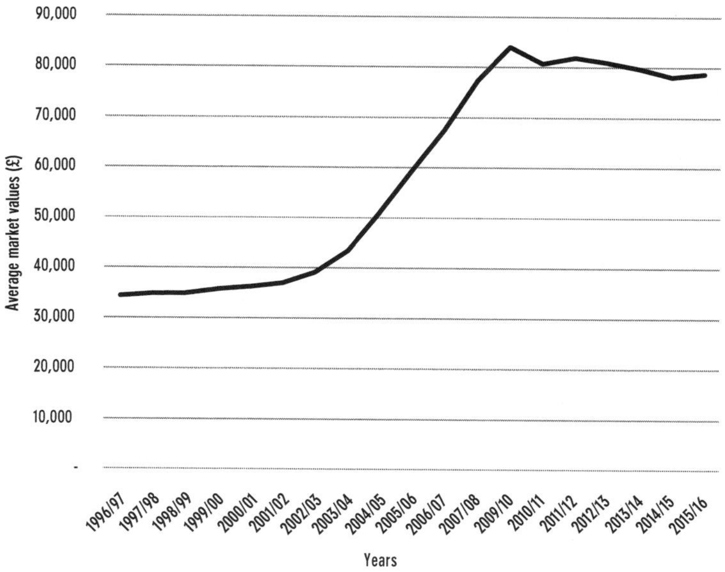

Source: Scottish Government live tables/sales to sitting tenants

inflation of house prices and the increased capacity of lenders before and after deregulation (the Building Societies Act 1986) had the effect of increasing building societies' participation in lending and contributing to a higher level of capital receipts for government. By the mid-1980s building societies and other private lenders had effectively removed the need for local authorities to lend.

Unlike other privatisations, the Right to Buy was not a short-lived sensation, but rather involved a steady recruitment of tenants whose circumstances and opportunities changed so that they chose to buy at a later stage. This meant that the policy generated a steady flow of capital receipts in almost every one of the years between 1980 and 2015, and the data in Table 4.6 indicates that over this period they generated in excess of £58 billion. Between 1981/82 and 2007/08, capital receipts in Great Britain exceeded £1 billion in every year.

Changing tenures

In 1980, when the legislation to provide the Right to Buy was introduced, council housing accounted for some 31% of all dwellings in the UK. Housing associations accounted for a further 2% of dwellings. From this date onwards both the numbers and share of council housing declined because of stock transfers as well as the Right to Buy. Housing associations experienced the opposite: both the number of dwellings and the share of the market rose initially because increased capital grants provided for new building and, subsequently, through transfers of stock from local authorities. But this growth had stalled by 2012 as cuts in government funding for housing capital programmes took effect. Council housing declined and housing associations grew across the different nations comprising the UK (see Table 4.7). By 2015 the stock of secure council tenancies eligible for the Right to Buy was less than 2.2 million in the UK – some 34% of the number at the time the Right to Buy was introduced. Councils and housing associations together owned just under 5 million dwellings – 70% of the combined total of social housing in 1980. After 35 years, in spite of the popularity

Table 4.6: Capital receipts from the sale of public housing in Great Britain, 1980-2014 (£ million cash)

Year	Receipts from sales			
	England and Wales			Scotland
	Local authorities	New towns	Total	
1980/81	692	44	736	
1981/82	1,394	60	1,454	
1982/83	1,981	69	2,050	
1983/84	1,499	77	1,576	
1984/85	1,269	74	1,343	
1985/86	1,209			
1986/87	1,408	63	1,471	
1987/88	1,922	89	2,011	
1988/89	3,020	128	3,148	
1989/90	3,153	123	3,276	
1990/91	1,945	60	2,005	882
1991/92	1,379	43	1,422	592
1992/93	1,135	28	1,163	485
1993/94	1,305	30	1,335	520
1994/95	1,239	30	1,269	361
1995/96	896	22	918	359
1996/97	964	4	968	337
1997/98	1,200	–	1,200	446
1998/99	1,148	–	1,148	476
1999/00	1,650	–	1,650	563
2000/01	1,704	–	1,704	540
2001/02	1,851	–	1,851	480
2002/03	2,615	–	2,615	515
2003/04	3,378	–	3,378	404
2004/05	2,988	–	2,988	185
2005/06	1,906	–	1,906	117
2006/07	1,521	–	1,521	42

Year	Receipts from sales			
	England and Wales			Scotland
	Local authorities	New towns	Total	
2007/08	1,214	–	1,214	18
2008/09	372	–	372	51
2009/10	257	–	257	13
2010/11	303		303	6
2011/12	250		250	7
2012/13	430		430	105
2013/14	827		827	
Total	50,024	993	51,018	7,504

Source: Forrest and Murie (1988) and Wilcox (various years)

of the Right to Buy and repeated government efforts to promote it, the UK had a large social rented sector, by international standards. This general picture applies to the different nations of the UK, although important differences remained. By 2008 housing associations had overtaken local authorities as the principal providers of not-for-profit or social rented housing in England (see Figure 4.6), and in Wales, but in Scotland and Northern Ireland, their contribution remained smaller than public sector landlords. Although Scotland had started with a much larger public sector (54% in 1980 compared with 31% in England) and experienced a lower take-up of Right to Buy in the years immediately after 1980, the sector saw a dramatic decline thereafter. There was a considerable convergence in the shares of public and social rented housing in England and Scotland, and by 2013, the difference was seven percentage points (24% in Scotland and 17% in England).

Table 4.7: Changes in tenure, 1971-2013

		1971	1980	1991	2001	2011	2013
England	**Dwellings (000s)**	16,065	17,864	19,838	21,310	23,039	23,436[c]
		%	%	%	%	%	%
	Council[a]	28	29	20	14	8	7
	Housing association	–	2	3	7	10	10
Scotland	**Dwellings (000s)**	1,822	1,997	2,160	2,312	2,495	2,521
		%	%	%	%	%	%
	Public	52	54	38	24	13	13
	Housing association	–	–	3	6	11	11
Wales	**Dwellings (000s)**	960	1,068	1,184	1,275	1,384	1,394
		%	%	%	%	%	%
	Public	28	29	19	15	6	6
	Housing association	–	–	2	4	10	10
Great Britain	**Dwellings (000s)**	18,999	20,929	23,146	24,897	26,918	27,224
		%	%	%	%	%	%
	Public[a]	31	31	22	15	8	8
	Housing association	–	2	3	6	10	10
Northern Ireland	**Dwellings (000s)**	425	494	573	668[b]	759	767[c]
		%	%	%	%	%	%
	NIHE	35	39	29	18	13	12
	Housing association	–	–	2	3	4	4
UK	**Dwellings (000s)**	19,259	21,423	23,719	25,571	27,677	27,987
		%	%	%	%	%	%
	Public[a]	31	31	22	15	8	8
	Housing association	–	2	3	6	10	10

Notes: 'Public' includes local authorities, new towns, Scottish Homes (and the Scottish Special Housing Association)
[a] Includes other public sector; [b] 2002; [c] 2014.
Source: Wilcox et al (2015).

Figure 4.6: Tenure change in England, 1969-2015

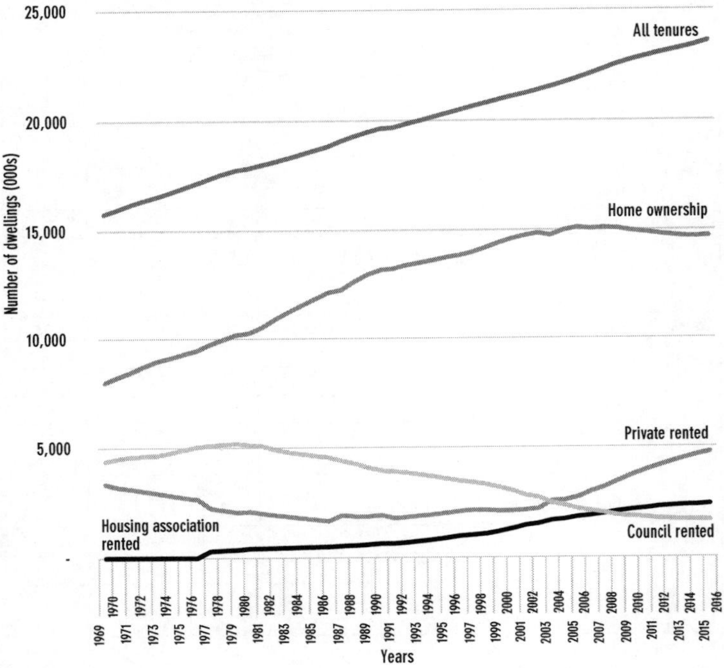

Source: DCLG Live Tables Table 104

Conclusions

The Right to Buy formed a key factor that contributed to the transformation of the tenure structure across the UK between 1980 and 2015. Sales fluctuated but were sustained at a high level throughout all but the end of the period. They reshaped the public sector, but also changed the home ownership sector, with more lower-value properties and flats in places that had previously been council estates. The favourable treatment of housing associations saw them grow steadily and they overtook councils as the main providers of social rented housing in England. These changes were much more significant and sustained than some commentators had anticipated, and the concerns about how they would affect access to housing were larger as a result. The cumulative and long-term consequences were also affected by the uneven pattern of sales, especially at a local and neighbourhood level. While national and regional differences tended to diminish, local differences remained.

Alongside consistently high levels of Right to Buy sales there were high average levels of discounts, and the cash value of these and the capital receipts generated by the Right to Buy raise a number of questions. First, they demonstrate the different cash discounts generated by the same policy formula. Accidents of time, property type and size and place translated into very different levels of benefit, and are more typical of a lottery than a policy associated with fairness. Second, they raise questions about proportionality. The average cash value of discounts in England was in excess of £20,000 throughout, and by 2013/14 was over £60,000. There were tenant purchasers receiving well above these averages. In contrast, other households seeking to buy a property were much less generously treated by the government. Was the disparity in levels of support reasonable, and were levels of Right to Buy discount proportionate? Finally, with over £58 billion of capital receipts from the Right to Buy, the capacity for reinvestment in housing or what began to be referred to as replacement was considerable. The failure to prioritise this before 1997 is striking, and questions remain about why more could not have been done over the whole period. The failure to reinvest in a period of major housing, demographic, social and economic change represents a lost opportunity, and forms part of the explanation for the housing crisis in later years.

5
A POLICY COMMENTARY

Introduction

The Right to Buy was initially advantageous to long established tenants who had no plans to move, but as the policy matured and discounts increased, the properties sold and the tenants buying changed – more purchasers had shorter tenancy histories and bought in order to move home. While the decision to buy proved beneficial for most purchasers, the advantages gained varied according to when and where people bought. The risks associated with changing health, employment and relationships could also lead to arrears and repossessions. Right to Buy buyers were more likely than buyers generally to be in insecure occupations and to experience difficulties with mortgages, in spite of the financial buffer provided by generous discounts. And the problems experienced with defective and unmortgageable properties and related to leasehold sales were only partly addressed by policy measures.

The longer-term effects are critically about whether Right to Buy properties remain owner-occupied once their original tenant purchasers move on. Do the properties remain in home ownership (housing first-time buyers or existing homeowners)? Or are properties transferred to other tenures, in which case the expansion of home ownership was temporary? What are the implications for how the policy worked in strategic and public expenditure terms? The loss of relets, failure to reinvest capital receipts in replacement housing, the benefit costs associated with transfers to private renting, issues about the condition of the housing stock sold under the Right to Buy and the impact at an estate level all connect with current housing problems and policies, access to housing and the use and targeting of public funds.

The Right to Buy – who was most likely to buy?

A body of research, over more than 40 years, has established the characteristics of purchasers of council dwellings under both the Right to Buy and previous discretionary policies (Murie, 1975; Niner, 1976; Forrest and Murie, 1984a, 1984b, 1988, 1990a; Kerr, 1988; Lynn, 1991; Foulis, 1985; NIHE, 1992; Holmans, 1993; Jones and Murie, 1999, 2006; Burrows et al, 2000; Marsh et al, 2003; Jones, 2003; Rowlands and Murie, 2008). This suggests continuities but also changes in the characteristics and intentions of purchasers. In the early years of the Right to Buy purchasers had similar characteristics to those who had bought council houses under discretionary policies, before 1980. Purchasers were still predominantly long established tenants who wanted to continue to live in their family home. Typical buyers were households of two or more adults, in the middle of the family life cycle, aged from 45 up to retirement age, with grown-up children that had often left home; they were employed with one or more earners, and in white-collar, skilled or semi-skilled occupations with incomes that were generally below the average, but higher than council tenants' incomes.

Early purchasers tended to live in the most attractive council dwellings and estates – partly reflecting how their neighbourhood had been shaped by themselves and their neighbours – and buying was seen as ultimately cheaper than renting. Households that were significantly under-represented among purchasers in the early stage included the youngest and oldest tenants, households with pre-school children, single-person households, unemployed people, female-headed households, lone-parent families and those in the lowest paid and unskilled jobs. Non-buyers were more concentrated in the least desirable parts of the council stock – flats and maisonettes and houses on the least popular estates. They had the least incentive and fewest resources to buy. The main reasons for not purchasing included 'being too old or having insufficient incomes' or were associated with living in a flat rather than a house.

The types of tenants in the first wave continued to be recruited to the Right to Buy in later years as households, whose incomes and family commitments had not enabled them to buy earlier, exercised the Right to Buy as family and employment circumstances changed. However, by the mid-1980s, the mix of properties sold, and of purchasers, was extended. Purchasers in this second wave of sales reflected the shifting balance of opportunity created by higher discounts, especially for flats, and changes in the economic and housing context. More young households bought and the proportion of older households and those with 20 years of tenancy was lower. By the 1990s Right to Buy purchasers were no longer so exclusively long established tenants wanting to secure their future in the family home and reschedule payment for it, but included a significant group with shorter periods of tenancy and less attachment to the home and neighbourhood. In the early 2000s the largest group of purchasers was aged between 35 and 45, were two-parent families with children at school, and they generally continued to have incomes below the national average, even for those in work.

When the Right to Buy was introduced, nearly half of purchasers had lived in their home for 20 years, but by 2002 buyers were most likely to have been living in the property for between six and ten years. Some purchasers were still the longstanding tenants that the policy had been aimed at, but others had been in council housing for much shorter periods. The tendency for more new buyers to want to move from their address in the near future appears to have increased into the 2000s. The majority (75%) of those aged under 35 wanted to move compared with only 33% of those aged 55 or over. Although the lowest income group was the least likely to wish to move, the moderate income group were more likely to want to move than the highest income group.

The evidence suggests a shift in the balance of motivations for buying. Some (but by no means all) of the later buyers, and especially younger households, purchased with the intention of moving on. The Right to Buy provided access to asset ownership that would enable trading within the market. Those wanting to move referred to changes in the area and a deterioration of living conditions, wanting more space, more bedrooms or a house rather than a flat or bungalow. Some of this reflects the increased range of properties and locations included in later sales. The reputation of council housing, poor services and facilities on estates and limited opportunities to move to better housing within the council sector also affected decisions. Not all tenants who chose not to buy were unable to: some had previously been homeowners and had credit rating or other issues that deterred them from buying again; others did not want to buy the property they lived in because of its size, type or condition and wanted to move, rather than be tied down by buying.

The profile of purchasers changed over the life of the Right to Buy. Arguably it started out broadly matching the expressed aims of policy – to reward longstanding tenants who had paid rent for years – and it enabled tenants who were committed to their home and neighbourhood to change tenure and to acquire an asset. The impact on neighbourhood and relets was negligible or positive as the households who bought did not intend to move and did not do so. In later years the policy rewarded households that had paid rent for a much shorter period (especially in leasehold properties) and appealed to households with ambitions to move. The Right to Buy became a reason for becoming a council tenant and, even when the household wanted to move, exercising the Right to Buy before giving up the tenancy made sense financially. Buying to facilitate residential movement and reselling as soon as there would be no penalty became more common and had a greater impact on relets and neighbourhoods. Higher discounts had unintended consequences that affected the dynamics of council housing and changed applicant and tenant behaviour. It also contributed to the development of a resale market attractive to private landlords.

Financial advantages and risks for purchasers

Any policy change arguably involves winners and losers. With the Right to Buy the winners were easily identifiable. Tenants who bought their housing generally gained significant benefits, and discounts reduced the risk compared with households buying on the open market. Where the Right to Buy did not generate long-term advantages, this was often because of other changes affecting the household (employment, health, relationship breakdown). These were not evidently 'failures' in the Right to Buy although they demonstrate that in some cases, being an owner left households more at risk of losing their home in periods of crisis and changing circumstances – remaining as a tenant meant some households were better able to cope with such changes.

Nevertheless, some Right to Buy purchasers experienced financial difficulties. They were more susceptible to unemployment, and to debt and housing problems (Jones, 2003). As the Right to Buy policy matured, many purchasers could not obtain standard mortgages, and some relied on 'sub-prime' finance because they could not certify their income, had County Court Judgments against them or had significant arrears. The extent of mortgage problems was affected by the interplay between borrowers' financial circumstances, the level of interest rates and lenders' practices. Borrowers who bought from a council or housing association were two to three times more likely to fall into arrears than someone with a standard mortgage (FSA, 2009). An unusually large number of Right to Buy purchasers were identified as in arrears or facing repossession – including older people, those with long-term health issues, or with large debt commitments, and those who had not taken the additional costs of housing repair and maintenance into account (Shelter, 2012). Evidence from Citizens' Advice Bureaux indicated that many borrowers had persistent low incomes, little knowledge of financial products and were vulnerable because of their age, state of mental health, physical disability, literacy or language difficulties (Tutton and Edwards, 2007). In spite of this evidence, the majority of Right to Buy purchasers did not experience insurmountable difficulties over mortgage payments.

Substantial discounts often provided scope for rescheduling payments or remortgaging to avert the threat of repossession.

One argument in favour of the Right to Buy was that it redistributed wealth from the state directly to sitting tenants, increasing the proportion of the population with substantial assets: the accumulated discounts on purchases accounted for an equity of £150-200 billion, representing 3-4% of total wealth (Hills et al, 2013). Three notes of caution have been expressed over this calculation, however. First, the right to a flow of subsidy associated with below market rents represents wealth and enables households to save. In this perspective, council tenants are wrongly portrayed as without any wealth, and the net transfer of wealth has to be adjusted in the light of this. Second (and as with the wealth associated with the rights to a tenancy), the asset may not be realisable during the owner's lifetime and is effectively tied up in providing housing – especially where low market values are involved. Third, financial gains from exercising the Right to Buy varied enormously according to what property was bought and where – the same policy generated enormously different returns. In terms of ongoing housing costs, the gap between rents and mortgage payments on discounted properties was often small, especially in periods of rising real rents. For those who purchased, this meant diminishing payments, and ultimately no mortgage payments at all, instead of continuing to pay rent for the rest of their lives.

The most positive experiences in these terms were not associated with how long someone had been a tenant but with accidents of time and place – for example, being able to purchase acquired street properties in high price areas of London. The contrast with a similar household living in a low price area is profound. While the former household could find that purchase increased their capacity to move home, property values for the latter were less likely to increase such opportunities. Issues of fairness emerge when an apparently uniform policy operates in such an uneven market. This underlines the importance of local housing market dynamics in shaping the differential effects of Right to Buy. Unskilled workers, those of working age who were economically dependent, and low-income households, all under-represented among Right to Buy purchasers, did not share in wealth redistribution.

The most negative experiences in relation to the Right to Buy were those associated with the purchase of properties that have subsequently proved difficult to sell or have high costs over and above mortgage repayments. Where lenders provided loans for the initial Right to Buy purchase (large discounts enormously reduced the risk), they were sometimes reluctant to finance subsequent sales, especially medium and high-rise properties and of non-traditional construction, when no discount was available, and this affected the resale of Right to Buy properties.

Leaseholder issues

The Right to Buy has generated unanticipated problems associated with its design and implementation rather than the characteristics of purchasers. When the policy was introduced, houses with gardens formed the bulk of council housing, and there was very little in their design that made individual ownership problematic. However, maisonettes and flats (including converted street properties) involved shared entries and other amenities and shared maintenance and repair responsibilities. In some cases heating, lifts and other facilities had been designed for collective (rather than individual) use, operation and financing. These arrangements were easy to manage when properties were all let as council tenancies, and any major capitalised repairs were financed, as initial construction costs had been, through borrowing that was slowly repaid through rents. Local authorities' discretionary sales policies tended to exclude these property types, but their sale as leasehold properties, under the Right to Buy in England and Wales, left the local authority, as freeholder, with continuing responsibilities (under English law) for management of the block, including maintenance of the external fabric, common areas and services and insurance. The lease agreement usually made provision for any costs the freeholder incurred in carrying out these responsibilities, to be recovered through charges levied on individual leaseholders based on their share of total costs as set out in their lease. Annual charges would be made for day-to-day management and maintenance and one-off charges for major works.

Major works charges (say, for replacing roofs or windows, external recladding or lift replacement) could be very substantial, and leaseholders' statutory rights related to how landlords discharged their responsibilities enabled them to challenge service and major works bills – landlords were required to consult leaseholders on work costing over £250. In addition, when a tenant was buying under the Right to Buy (and the Right to Acquire or Social HomeBuy), the landlord had to provide a five-year estimate of the service charge payable, including the cost of any planned major works, and could not charge more than this estimate during the first five years of the lease, except to take account of inflation. There was no special limit on charges for repairs carried out after the first five years.

The issues that subsequently arose over the management of Right to Buy leasehold properties were not anticipated. Neither local authorities nor central government could draw on significant expertise or experience to offer advice, and leases differed. Most local authorities could have been criticised for some failings over how they managed properties in the decade after 1980. They had no significant previous experience in this area. It was costly to develop specialist leasehold management services, and this was not a priority while there were few leaseholders. They were slow to develop robust, professional approaches. But the issue was more complex, and neither Right to Buy leasehold purchasers nor their advisers (including solicitors) were well informed about service charges (Forrest et al, 1995b). If there was awareness that they would be liable for service charges, leaseholders often had unrealistic expectations about the costs of managing properties and of major works. This situation changed slowly, as local authorities and housing associations gained experience and their leasehold properties increased. New leases were also unlikely to have the degree of ambiguity that had sometimes existed previously.

From the mid-1980s there was a stream of complaint, controversy, consultation and initiatives concerning Right to Buy leaseholds.

Ministers and Members of Parliament were bombarded with cases, and 'excessive' service charges proved popular press stories. Responses were forthcoming from the government, but measures introduced to help leaseholders in 1995, 2007 and again in 2010 always failed to satisfy leaseholders. Social landlords were left with powers and duties related to charging for works and providing assistance to leaseholders. They could help leaseholders to pay their bills by using their discretion to reduce bills, by providing loans, offering equity release products, allowing leaseholders to pay their bills by monthly instalments over an extended period, or deferring payment until the property was sold. Local authorities also had powers to buy back properties from owners in financial difficulties. Most local authorities and housing associations with leasehold properties in England eventually developed highly professional practices and leasehold management improved. But the legal position, and options and practices in leasehold management, was complex and often remained confusing for leaseholders and their advisers. Conflicts could also arise where leaseholders wanted to minimise short-term costs while the landlord and tenants were had longer-term objectives related to quality of repairs and value for money.

The legacy of Right to Buy leasehold sales was the continuing entanglement of government in the financing and detailed regulation of part of the housing system. Faced with a disenchanted leaseholder lobby and dramatic real examples, governments intervened to adopt measures for social sector leaseholders that were not extended to other leaseholders. Some measures sheltered Right to Buy leaseholders (but not open market purchasers) from the full financial consequences of their decision to buy. This was not the expectation in a privatisation programme designed to leave households to face the risks and opportunities afforded by private ownership. Privatisation left the government with continuing and important tasks related to housing. By 2016 some councils (especially London boroughs and city councils) and housing associations had a major leasehold management role that did not exist in 1980. Furthermore, their role was increasingly concerned with management of properties bought on the open market rather than under the Right to Buy, and with leaseholders who had not previously been council tenants.

Abuses of the Right to Buy

The Right to Buy was intended to enable tenants to become homeowners, and discounts were designed to assist tenants to achieve this and not to enable tenants or others to make speculative gains. The acknowledged abuses of the Right to Buy arose where these intentions were subverted, tenants were not buying to become homeowners and stay in the property, and third parties with no rights under the legislation sought to gain from it. From the outset (and under previous discretionary policies) it was evident that people other than the sitting tenants drove some purchases. Family members who encouraged or financed the purchase increased completions. In cases where this resulted in tenants staying as owners wholly or partly funded by their family, this presented no obvious problem, but sometimes family members wanting to sell the property and cash in put pressure on the purchaser to move.

The most developed abuses, however, emerged during the later 1990s, when booming house prices and estate modernisation provided opportunities that were seized on by property companies and others. The clearest examples involved tenants purchasing under the Right to Buy after having entered into agreements to sell their home to a third party. These became a cause for concern along with questions about the impact of the Right to Buy on the regeneration of council-built estates: applications under the Right to Buy triggered by plans for major restructuring, including demolition, could be considerably delayed and costs increased. Jones' (2003) account of third party abuses refers to areas and property types where resale markets had not been established because of low demand, or because mainstream lenders were reluctant to provide mortgages for dwellings with non-traditional construction including medium and high-rise flats. Owners of these properties experienced difficulties in selling, and the prices that could be realised were low – with many eventually sold at auction for knock-down prices to investors. Landlords, including small private companies, who specialised in holding portfolios of properties where there were weak markets, targeted inner-city and some council-built neighbourhoods.

The poor investment prospects in these areas were a deterrent to the exercise of the Right to Buy, but in some cases, private property companies acquired former council housing from Right to Buy purchasers. Forward sale and lease arrangements were agreed: the company funded the Right to Buy purchase and council tenants received a cash lump sum that was considerably below the value of the discount. The company had immediate control and long-term ownership of the dwelling, and offered it to rent. Jones indicated as many as 20 companies, set up in the late 1990s, actively operating such schemes, almost exclusively in inner London where maximum discounts were highest and demand was high.

According to the companies, between 60 and 70% of the tenants who entered into these agreements planned to move away from London. The practice had very different effects from the stated intention of the policy, and rewarded speculative purchasers and tenants who did not intend to stay in the property. The companies stated that the properties involved were let at low rents (for central London), mainly to young (foreign) professionals, 'key' workers and students. Some were leased to housing associations, local authorities and government agencies dealing with asylum-seekers.

The volume of activity under these schemes is difficult to ascertain, and Jones (2003) suggested a figure in the low thousands over the peak four-year period of its existence – some 6% of Right to Buy sales per year in inner London. Subsequent market conditions and the lower maximum discounts available before 2010 made these schemes less viable – but increased maximum discounts after 2010 are likely to have revived such schemes.

Longer-term consequences: resales and access to housing

From the outset, discussion of the Right to Buy acknowledged that once sold, public and social rented dwellings would no longer be relet by social landlords. The next occupier of the dwelling would be selected through a market process – by who bought the property on resale or how its private sector owner selected a tenant. There would be a loss of relets by the original landlord, and the way access to housing was negotiated would change. While this much was accepted, its significance was disputed. Some argued that, when resold, Right to Buy properties would command low prices and be accessible, and the experience of discretionary sales suggested that immediate loss of relets would be very small. The profile and motives of early Right to Buy purchasers supported the view that few tenants who bought would have moved: their properties would not have become available for letting for a considerable time and the immediate loss of relets was small.

The champions of the policy focused on the good news for purchasers and the longer-term loss of relets was generally ignored. But after 30 years, the loss of relets has built up (as Right to Buy purchasers aged and households have been dissolved) – and at a faster rate because of the different characteristics of later purchasers who were more inclined to move. The evidence relating to the loss of relets is initially about the rate at which Right to Buy properties were resold. In England the average resale rate was 14% by 1991 after 10 years of Right to Buy with variation between 8 and 30% in 35 different local authority areas (Forrest et al, 1995a). Resale rates were greater in the higher priced areas in the South of England. In Northern Ireland 10% of all dwellings sold by the Housing Executive to sitting tenants had been resold on the open market by 1991 (NIHE, 1992). In Scotland, in the first decade of Right to Buy, around 10% of dwellings sold under Right to Buy by the Scottish Special Housing Association (SSHA) had been resold (Twine and Williams, 1991, 1993), and by 1997 22% of Right to Buy properties in Scotland had been resold (67,000 dwellings); within that total, 25,000 had been sold twice or more (Pawson et al, 1997). Later studies have suggested that as time has passed since the original sale, the rate of resale has increased.

What emerges is that expectations of a slow initial rate of sale were correct. In the short term, if the same household continued to live in the same property, there was no displacement or lost opportunity for someone else to become a tenant. In these circumstances Right to Buy represented the transfer of property from one tenure to another, with little net impact on access to housing. It is an overstatement to suggest that there was no immediate loss of relets and the changing profile of purchasers and properties resulted in a greater medium-term loss of relets than anticipated.

Nevertheless, the most significant impact of Right to Buy on housing access occurred after a considerable time. The number of new council lettings declined sharply: from 221,000 in 2000/01 to 83,000 in 2013/14. This was because of the decline in the size of the council sector as a result of stock transfers and Right to Buy sales. At this stage, the key issue is whether the loss of relets matters: irrespective of when Right to Buy dwellings were resold, were they bought by households with characteristics similar to new or existing tenants in the social rented sector? If purchasers had the same resources and other characteristics as households entering social rented housing, then the impact of Right to Buy on housing access could be regarded as negligible – access was through a different process and to a different tenure, but the outcome, in terms of dwelling obtained, was essentially the same.

The evidence shows that some former council properties provided a route for first-time buyers but others enabled homeowners who already owned lower-priced homes to trade up in size, space and quality. Although former council houses were generally priced below properties of equivalent size, age and type, they were larger and better than properties that formed the bottom of the market (Forrest and Murie, 1990b; Twine and Williams, 1993). In England 51% of Right to Buy resales were bought by homeowners, and the proportion of former homeowners was 48% in the North, 47% in the Midlands/ South West and 58% in the South. In the higher house price areas of the South of England, former council housing commanded prices likely to be beyond the reach of first-time buyers, and the proportion of purchasers who were existing owners was consequently higher (Forrest et al, 1995a).

Some 35% of first-time purchasers were newly formed households. The remainder were established, independent households moving from (mainly private) rented accommodation. The evidence for Scotland (Twine and Williams, 1993; Pawson et al; 1997; Pawson and Watkins, 1998) and Northern Ireland (NIHE, 2001) shows a similar variation in the characteristics of resale purchasers, but resold properties were more likely to form the bottom of the market and more likely to be bought by first-time buyers.

Because lower-quality private properties – poor quality flat conversions and pre-1919 terraced houses, for example – were smaller and in poorer condition, less well-designed and built, with tiny gardens, they provided the bottom end of the housing market. Where house prices were generally lower, former council properties were more likely to be accessible to first-time buyers with some similar characteristics to households that had previously sought to rent council houses. In the South of England prices commanded by some former council houses were strikingly above those that applied to flats and to smaller properties in the private sector. In the Midlands and the North of England, however, this price difference was not so striking, and the results are comparable with those for Scotland and Northern Ireland. All the studies showed the balance between continuing owners and first-time purchasers varied, and suggest that the role of former council housing in the market reflects local and regional levels of demand, differences in quality and condition of former council houses and comparisons with private sector homes. In all cases, because of the higher space and quality standards required in the public sector, former council homes were superior in quality and larger than some private sector properties.

In areas of high housing demand, a higher proportion of buyers of former council dwellings were households with heads in professional or managerial employment and existing owners. In Mole Valley in

Kent, 73% of Right to Buy purchasers were existing homeowners and more than half were in higher status occupations. In Northern England there were higher proportions of purchasers in manual work and fewer existing homeowners. For example, in Knowsley, only a quarter of purchasers were existing owners (Forrest et al, 1995a). The proportion of Right to Buy resale purchasers originating from the public sector was also affected by local tenure structures. The average figure for England was 15%, including households that were either tenants or children of tenants. In Glasgow 49% of resale purchasers had been public sector tenants (Jones and Murie, 1999). Some one in five of the owner-occupiers who bought Right to Buy resales in Scotland had previously owned former council dwellings with the majority having bought through the Right to Buy (Pawson et al, 2002).

Studies over a number of years in different locations indicate that resale purchasers were typically young couples with or without children, with at least one full-time earner in skilled manual, professional or managerial employment. Households were concentrated in the 25-39 age group, and in England (Forrest et al, 1995a) over a quarter of heads of household were in professional or managerial jobs, with almost 40% in white-collar employment. More than a third had more than one earner in the household. Purchasers in the South of England, where prices were higher, were more likely to be childless, two-income professional workers, while purchasers in the North included more families and households on low incomes. The characteristics of these resale purchasers mean that the original Right to Buy purchasers from the 1980s were being replaced by much younger households, many of whom intended to move on in the foreseeable future as their family changed.

The evidence suggests that while low-income council tenants have a route into home ownership through the Right to Buy, a much smaller group of similarly low-income households access home ownership through resales. Some of the former council stock is accessible only to higher-income households and former homeowners. This pattern holds everywhere for larger, more attractive houses with gardens, and especially in higher demand areas. The best former council housing on the best estates is increasingly beyond the reach of many households with characteristics that would previously have enabled them to become council tenants. The Right to Buy has changed patterns of access and social and spatial patterns associated with housing. Lower-income households, irrespective of whether or not they are in work, are less able to access the best quality council-built housing and more likely to find their opportunities restricted to less attractive dwellings irrespective of tenure. The association between where people live and what they live in and their occupation and income has become stronger. In some rural and other places, where demand is high and public and social rented housing always formed only a small share of housing, the consequences of changed patterns of access are particularly severe. Households with local work and family connections are unable to buy a property in competition with others who do not have the same local links. In these areas, the supply of 'homes for locals' has been affected.

From the Right to Buy to private renting

The Right to Buy was a policy to expand home ownership. The context for the debates about council house sales leading up to 1979 was one of long-term, arguably terminal, decline of private renting across the UK. The Right to Buy was designed to extend opportunities for home ownership and, insofar as there was a debate about resales and how the market would adjust in the long term, the implicit assumption was that, once privatised, the former council stock would remain owner-occupied. While the wider housing policy agenda, consistently pursued after 1979, included deregulation of both private renting and of banks and building societies, there was limited evidence of any effective revival of private renting before the early 2000s. Consequently, the continuing debate about the Right to Buy neglected the interface with private renting. As has been indicated previously, resales of Right to Buy dwellings increased through the 1990s, and it seems likely that an increasing proportion of these resales were bought by investors for private letting. This is partly associated with the types of properties involved, but also reflects the working through of deregulation and the growth of Buy to Let mortgage products.

The initial evidence of Right to Buy resales in England (Forrest et al, 1995a) indicated that almost 8% of the originally sold Right to Buy dwellings had become privately rented after a decade: out of 151,000 resales, 12,000 had become privately rented. Among these resales, 17% of private rented properties were flats compared with only 4% of owner-occupied properties. Households that were renting former council homes from private landlords were more likely to be single, living in large adult households and aged under 25 (Forrest et al, 1995a). In Scotland, by 2002, when 37% of all Right to Buy property had been resold, 6% of resales had become privately rented (Scottish Executive, 2006).

Later surveys indicated much higher levels of private renting among former Right to Buy dwellings. This probably reflects both the general expansion of that tenure since 2001, and the increase in the rate of resales as the cohort of early Right to Buy purchasers aged, and more flats and other lower value properties offering attractive opportunities for private investors came onto the market. Jones indicated that in inner London, three years after the Right to Buy sale, only 74% of households living in former council housing were the original Right to Buy purchasers: more than 25% of Right to Buy properties had become privately rented (Jones, 2003). Much lower figures applied elsewhere, with only 7% privately rented in Birmingham, 6% in Havering and 3% in Leeds.

In Birmingham, analysis of census data showed that by 2001, each of 12 identified council estates had seen a considerable growth in privately rented property – at least partly attributable to transfers of Right to Buy properties to private renting. In the extreme case, within the council estate area identified in Ladywood, the decline in the social rented sector was 27 percentage points, while the private rented sector had grown by 43%. There was no other possible source for the growth of private renting other than the stock that had been sold through the Right to Buy. While the initial sales of council properties generated growth in home ownership, resales resulted in a decline in home ownership. Rather than creating mixed social rented/home ownership estates, what has been created was mixed social rented/private rented or social rented/private rented/home ownership estates.

Because of the importance of this issue a more detailed account is provided of research in Birmingham that indicated further significant change by 2011 (Bentley et al, 2014). Birmingham City Council has records of properties sold under the Right to Buy and earlier discretionary policies, but there is no data identifying the current tenure of these individual addresses. The population census provides data for output areas, and the analysis reported here refers to groupings of super output areas that include an average of some 500-600 dwellings but do not exactly match the boundaries of council estates. Examination of these data enables the identification of tenure change at this area level, and its interpretation can take into account the limitations of the data.

Analysis of 2011 census and council house sales data for the whole city identified nine areas where sold council properties accounted for over 20% of dwellings, and where private renting accounted for over 20% of dwellings in 2011. In all of these areas there had been a decline in social rented housing and a growth in private renting between 2001 and 2011. Six of the areas had also experienced a decline in home ownership. These data establish that there has been a significant growth of private renting in areas with a high number of council house sales. In seven of the nine areas the numbers of private rented dwellings exceeded the number of council dwellings in 2011, and in three of the nine areas identified, the number of homeowners was lower than the number of sold council dwellings. Even if all of the homeowners lived in former council dwellings (rather than other adjacent properties), there had been a transfer to private renting with the highest rates being between 22 and 31%.

While we can be confident that there have been significant transfers of former council dwellings, both leasehold and freehold, to private renting, this is difficult to quantify precisely. The data suggest the minimum rate of transfer in these areas, and a 'cautious' estimate is that between 20 and 30% of Right to Buy properties had become privately rented by 2011, and that this was likely to increase. This is consistent with the findings of a succession of studies, nationally and locally. Private renting had expanded in council estates that had previously only had council or owner-occupied properties While the pace of growth of private renting was likely to be uneven, there were implications for the demand and delivery of a variety of services, especially where changes in tenure affect the demographics, dynamics and stability of neighbourhoods. There are also implications for incomes, household budgets and benefits associated with higher housing costs in the private rented sector.

Two influential reports on transfers of Right to Buy properties to private renting refer only to leasehold sales, and consequently may not indicate the pattern for Right to Buy properties in general. The first of these (Copley, 2014) found that some 36% of all Right to Buy leaseholds sold by councils across London were let by private landlords. Substantial numbers of Right to Buy properties in the private rented sector were being let to tenants receiving Housing Benefit. The second report (Apps, 2015) estimated that 38% of council homes sold as leaseholds under the Right to Buy were in the private rented sector. Ninety-one local authorities across England (but excluding many of the largest leasehold landlords) reported that, in 47,994 of the 127,763 flats and maisonettes sold under Right to Buy since 1980, leaseholders were 'living away from the property'. This suggests that the properties were being privately rented.

It is unclear how to extrapolate from these data. They are generally consistent with other data in terms of a rising trend and the level achieved, but the London market has distinctive elements likely to affect outcomes, and leasehold properties may be more prone to transfer to private renting. Various factors, including difficulties in obtaining mortgages, make some flats less attractive to homeowners, and the transfer to private renting may consequently be higher among these properties – and perhaps other lower-priced and less attractive properties. Nevertheless, it seems likely that 30-40% of former Right to Buy properties have become privately rented, with some much higher proportions at block or neighbourhood levels.

Housing Benefit costs after the Right to Buy

The growth of private renting in the former council stock demonstrates that the Right to Buy has failed to provide a sustainable mechanism for the expansion of home ownership. Properties were owner-occupied for a transitional period before becoming rented again, but in the private rather than public or social rented sector. But the resale to private landlords is also significant where the properties concerned are then let to households qualifying for Housing Benefit and, because of higher rents in the private sector, this involves higher public expenditure than would have been the case had the properties been let to the same households by social landlords.

While council housing had in the past also been subsidised directly by the Exchequer, the move to deficit subsidy had reduced this and removed it in most local authorities – in some cases, surpluses left them net contributors to the Exchequer. The most robust analysis of the Housing Benefit costs associated with former Right to Buy dwellings transferred to private renting was completed by Sprigings and Smith (2012) in Renfrewshire, matching individual data for Right to Buy sales (up to 2007) with Local Housing Allowance (LHA) payments of Housing Benefit to private tenants and the compulsory (but incomplete) register of private rented stock. Some 57% of council dwellings had been sold under the Right to Buy, and 1,526 of the 3,558 current LHA claims derived from former Right to Buy properties. This was 43% of all LHA claims, involving 9.4% of Right to Buy sales. The authors extrapolated from these figures to the UK market to estimate that, had these properties still been in the public sector and subject to the lower rents that applied there, a saving of £3.2 million per annum would have been made in Housing Benefit payments. In the long term a significant proportion of Right to Buy sales become privately rented, with some tenants eligible for higher levels of Housing Benefit (for market rents) than if the properties had remained in the social rented sector. Payments to subsidise these higher rents do not translate into new housing investment or well managed and maintained secure housing, and this highlights the longer-term unanticipated consequences of the Right to Buy.

Housing Benefit for private tenants cost £3 billion in 2003/04, but had increased to £9.2 billion by 2011/12. The increase in Housing Benefit expenditure is associated with deregulation of the private rented sector, the increase in the size of the sector, increased average payments and a shift in the caseload from the social rented to the private rented sector. Average weekly awards in the private rented sector are over £20 per week higher than in the social rented sector. This equates to over £1,000 per annum for each claim. If 40% of Right to Buy sales had become privately rented, this amounts to some 800,000 properties in the UK; the excess subsidy bill is then likely to be over £800 million annually. The shift in caseload to the private rented sector has partly been occasioned by shortages of social rented housing, and this, in turn, has been driven by the cumulative loss of relets and lack of replacement building. Local authorities have turned to the private sector to meet their statutory obligations to the homeless and to address the needs of vulnerable households.

One perspective is that the Right to Buy temporarily inflated the level of home ownership: substantial subsidies (discounted prices) inflated effective demand for house purchase. In subsequent transactions, at market prices, putative owner-occupiers have no equivalent subsidy and Buy to Let purchasers are willing and able to pay more. While the pace of growth of private renting in the Right to Buy resale sector is likely to be uneven, there are implications for the demand and delivery of services. These impacts will be particularly pronounced where changes in tenure affect the demographics, dynamics and stability of neighbourhoods. There are also implications for incomes, household budgets and benefits associated with higher housing costs in the private rented sector.

Housing estates and housing conditions

Where the Right to Buy was exercised there was an immediate change in the tenure of a dwelling and household, and in the way housing was paid for and managed. Otherwise, the dwelling, the household and the neighbourhood initially remained the same. After almost 2 million Right to Buy sales, 35 years, resales and different patterns of investment, there have been changes in both dwellings and estates.

The Right to Buy involved sales of a variety of property types and sizes, built at different times, in different locations. Some estates were very popular and had a low turnover while others were difficult to manage and to live in. Some public housing was over 50 years old and needed repair or replacement; other parts of the stock, and especially system-built and other non-traditional building forms, had major construction flaws or were affected by physical and social obsolescence. Had these properties remained in the public sector there would have been a major task of repair and improvement, and it is notable that concerns about both difficult-to-let housing and a backlog of disrepair were increasingly evident from the 1970s onwards, with a succession of programmes directed at them (including Estate Action, Housing Action Trusts and the Estate Renewal Challenge Fund). Some estates had very good and others less good reputations, and were in good (or poor) locations in terms of environment facilities, employment, access and other resources. The uneven pattern of sales and resales and of transfers to private renting affected a differentiated council sector, with properties and estates that were different in popularity, condition, turnover and management.

Against this background the impact of the Right to Buy was uneven. The image of homeowners as committed to their homes and tenants expecting the landlord to do everything was always inaccurate: change of tenure enabled many longstanding tenants who had already invested resources in their family home to consolidate and reaffirm existing housing and family strategies. What happened to estates would depend on the position of the estate and the property in the market, the extent to which purchasers were longstanding tenants buying to stay or households buying to move, the rate and timing of resale (and whether resale purchasers were homeowners or private landlords), turnover and the strategies pursued by local authorities and housing associations (including major repair, renewal and regeneration programmes and activity to achieve the Decent Homes standard). These factors distinguish estates according to their popularity and role in the market (including housing costs), tenure composition and access and management.

This book has noted the different rates of Right to Buy sales for different properties according to their dwelling type and size and when and where they were built. Attractive houses with gardens sold much more rapidly in the early years, and although flat sales increased after 1986, houses remained more likely to be sold. Because sales were greater on low density interwar and postwar suburban estates, council housing diminished significantly in these zones, and became proportionately greater in inner-city and outer-city areas associated with slum clearance redevelopment and the different construction techniques and property types favoured in the 1960s and 1970s.

Early data suggested that less popular and attractive estates, including estates with a high proportion of flats and non-traditionally built properties, had fewer Right to Buy sales, and even as some properties were sold on most estates, the uneven rate of sale remained. Households that have been allocated to social rented housing in more recent years were consequently were likely to be channelled towards these less popular estates rather than being dispersed more widely, because the availability of tenancies elsewhere had declined. This has tended to increase neighbourhood concentrations of disadvantaged and vulnerable households. Right to Buy sales on some less attractive estates also seem more likely to be resold quickly and to become privately rented.

While all council estates have been affected to some extent by Right to Buy, there is a divergence related to the rate of initial sale and pattern of subsequent sale. Ownership in some estates remains predominantly by the council or homeowners; others are becoming council or privately rented with declining home ownership; and others have a mix of three tenures. We lack good research evidence on this, but it is likely that, rather than reducing concentrations of deprivation by introducing tenure mix, the situation after the Right to Buy involves some estates with greater concentrations of deprivation, greater insecurity and less coherent management and capacity to address neighbourhood problems. There is a divergence in estate trajectories between estates in high price areas that have become 'gentrified' home ownership zones accessible mainly to affluent households, and other estates dominated by less popular social lettings and easy access private lettings and marked by high turnover and fragmented management. Between these extremes there are a variety of situations.

In 1980 the government dismissed the view that the Right to Buy would contribute to the residualisation of housing and leave a tenure that increasingly represented welfare housing (House of Commons, 1981). In the event it is evident that the Right to Buy speeded up an established trend for council housing to disproportionately house vulnerable and low-income groups and elderly and young households. As more affluent tenants bought and became homeowners, so the profile of public housing narrowed further. But at a neighbourhood level the pattern was not the same. Estates that emerged with higher levels of public and social renting mixed with significant private renting developed an increasingly narrow social base associated with deprivation, and the contrast with some other estates increased. Rather than the Right to Buy reducing concentrations of deprivation or introducing more social mix, it has introduced a new process generating polarisation and segregation. Lower-income and vulnerable households that are more dependent on renting have fewer opportunities to move to the better estates.

This pattern has been evidenced through 1981 and 2001 census data in Birmingham, where sale prices or affordability in 12 estates has diverged over time (Murie, 2008b; 2014). This suggests that privatisation does not immediately change the position of estates, but over the longer term market processes, including the growth of private renting, are likely to speed differentiation and segregation. The most important conclusion emerging from this relates to the worst estates. Privatisation through the Right to Buy will rarely revitalise the least attractive estates or increase diversity, and will make their regeneration more difficult.

The growth in private renting has meant that estates have a fragmented pattern of rental ownership, that tenants living within the estates have different rights, and that the dynamics of the estate and the problems of managing the estate intensify. The least desirable properties for homeowners may be flats within high-rise blocks, and partly because of this, their prices tend to be lower. They become attractive targets for private landlords who buy the properties and may sub-divide them by converting them into bedsits with shared use of a toilet and a kitchen. So a two-bedroom flat with a living room becomes three bedsits, generating three rent payments. The use of the flat, the noise associated with comings and goings, the amount of activity affecting neighbours, will be very different than was intended in the design of these properties. In this scenario, the management problems, rather than becoming less, are likely to become greater. This is most likely to occur in the least desirable estates. The scenario then is that the worst estates will revert back to rented estates (more difficult to manage because of fragmented ownership) while the best estates will remain mixed tenure.

After the Right to Buy differences in demand are reflected in house prices. But the position of properties within the market is essentially the same as when quality, location, condition and reputation affected demand within the public sector. Whether estates are public, private or mixed tenure, the poorest households tend to move to estates and properties with relatively low demand: more affluent households are more likely to access the better estates. In this sense privatisation does not break continuity in the position of estates within the housing market hierarchy of the city. The worst estates remain unattractive and the issues associated with them re-emerge within the market. However, because there is less social renting, some of the moderating influences, especially on the worst estates, are taken away. So the tendency for polarisation between estates in terms of their social profile, their ethnic profile, or how attractive they are to live in increases. Without social rented sector lettings to distort the market, where people live more closely reflects capacity to exercise choice and ability to pay.

The investment in property within the market will also relate to market position, so estates with more affluent households and with better prospects of achieving a higher sale price are likely to be better maintained and to attract more investment. Within the social rented sector this would not always be the case. Investments in maintenance and repair and refurbishment would be more likely to be politically controlled or on some planned maintenance cycle. Turnover and turbulence will reflect the role in the market and again, without the bureaucratic processes associated with the social rented sector, the instability of the worst estates is likely to get worse rather than better. Finally, within the market there will be a weaker direct management of the neighbourhood as the fragmented ownership of property means that there is no one responsible for managing the neighbourhood as a whole.

These differences result in divergent trajectories for estates, and mean that the worst estates do not improve. The questions raised about the consequences of the Right to Buy are greatest for the worst estates. At a neighbourhood level it is reasonable to argue that the best estates will become better. They may have a greater mix of households and there may be more investment in them. The downside of this is not at a neighbourhood level, but in the consequences for the households who are now no longer able to access these estates unless they have higher incomes. Privatisation of the better estates has adverse consequences on the opportunities of lower-income households, but deterioration of neighbourhood is more likely in those estates that are already difficult to live in and to manage.

Having sustained a policy that generates unequal outcomes at an estate level, there has been no coherent strategy to counteract the effect. In Scotland and Wales the suspension and abolition of the Right to Buy will prevent a further ratcheting of the concentration effect, but previous sales are not undone by this and the effect will remain. Across the UK there was a failure to embark on replacement investment that would have created more opportunities for social tenants, and a failure to sustain investment in repair, renewal and regeneration of estates.

While the Decent Homes policy was an ambitious, sector-wide programme of improvement it did not involve public sector housing renewal or regeneration. Other policies (Turkington and Watson, 2015) had some impact but were not maintained or rolled out to enough estates or combined with funds to enable sufficient public and social housing investment. The problems associated with the least attractive estates are not addressed by the sale of individual dwellings. They require policies to address regeneration, neighbourhood dynamics and management, and to increase the opportunities for households unable to access home ownership. If the resources released through privatisation were reinvested, especially in the worst estates, it is conceivable that privatisation could provide a mechanism that would improve more estates and have positive outcomes. This opportunity was missed with the Right to Buy policy in the UK.

To some extent this discussion can be summarised as indicating that where housing provision, investment and management is determined by market processes, the outcome will be more uneven than where it is determined by bureaucracies. Higher value, higher income areas attract more spending than other areas in a market system. This pattern also applies if reference is made to individual property condition. Where low-income households exercised a Right to Buy purchase, subsidised through discounts, this was affordable (albeit sometimes only just), but subsequent essential repairs might not be affordable – especially if purchasers' incomes fell. Purchasers' immediate actions after purchase often included cosmetic or more substantial expenditure to personalise and improve their home. In the early years of discretionary and Right to Buy sales, the sold properties often stood out because of new porches, windows and extensions.

Twenty or more years on, properties still owned by the council had been upgraded, and sold properties sometimes stood out because of their dilapidation, the lack of new roofs and gutters and with porches in need of replacement. Some issues about emerging disrepair arose as the cohort who were the first to buy aged – some increasingly elderly owners of Right to Buy properties experienced difficulty with repair and maintenance. The Right to Buy generated problems that were familiar in parts of the homeownership market. Evidence about house condition problems in Right to Buy properties does not suggest a crisis of house condition, but presents a reasonably consistent picture (Forrest and Murie, 1990b; Murie and Leather, 2000). Sold council properties, especially those still retained by the original purchasers, had higher average repair costs and were not in as good condition as properties still in public ownership, but had lower average repair costs and were in better condition than the mainstream owner-occupied stock. The variation in repair and maintenance (and so house condition) in Right to Buy properties is greater than within the social rented sector. At best, Right to Buy properties are in better condition, but at worst, they are in poorer condition. The more recent tendency for Right to Buy properties to become privately rented brings with it a risk of a decline in standards. Private rented homes are more likely than properties in other tenures to fail basic health and safety standards and fall below the Decent Homes standard.

The inclusion in the Right to Buy of non-traditionally built dwellings that proved unmortgageable because of construction defects led the government to introduce the Housing Defects Act 1984 to provide financial support for purchasers, and the government was obliged to divert public expenditure to prioritise costly remedial works to specific types of dwellings including Airey and Smith houses built in the immediate postwar years using prefabrication. This distorted local and national priorities for capital spending. Similar problems related to construction were not as widespread or as easily specified, and so were not recognised even though they affected resale and resale values. Leasehold properties also presented problems because of the costs of repairs and improvements. However, from a house condition perspective, the responsibilities remaining with public and social landlords for maintenance and repair ensured that major failings in these areas were avoided.

Conclusions

The debate about housing in 2016 is concerned with low rates of construction and other investment in housing, problems of access to home ownership, the quality and cost of privately rented housing, and increasing numbers of households experiencing homelessness and inadequate or inappropriate housing. Housing problems have increased since the Right to Buy, and are directly linked to the reduction in the size of the public and social rented sector and the failure to reinvest Right to Buy receipts in the housing sector. It is undeniable that the Right to Buy could have been implemented alongside an investment programme designed to neutralise its adverse effects, but without reinvestment to replace the loss of relets, serious shortages of affordable and accessible housing have emerged. The capital receipts from Right to Buy sales were not used for replacement or renewal, and current housing problems must be partly attributed to the failure to reinvest and to see the Right to Buy in the context of a wider strategy to address housing need as well as demand.

The Right to Buy in retrospect, and without any accompanying strategy for housing access and supply, represents a singular failure in strategic thinking. It has left a legacy of housing stress and shortage, high subsidy to private sector housing and housing inequality. Its strategic implications are also associated with its effect on the supply of purpose-built sheltered housing, housing for people with disabilities and housing in rural and other areas where there was only a small council and social housing stock. Measures designed to prevent the sale of purpose-built properties for older people or people with disabilities were put in place and had some impact – but other properties normally let to (but not purpose-built for) such groups were not excluded. In rural areas the loss of stock has been as rapid or more so, and planning-related measures and conditions restricting resale to locals have largely proved ineffective. In practice, and until measures related to pressured areas in Scotland and Wales, the protection of the supply of housing for locals added to the attraction of stock transfer, with its effect in limiting the Right to Buy to existing tenants.

Throughout its operation, Right to Buy exhortation highlighted short-term gains to individuals and neglected longer-term and strategic considerations. In the short term, there was no displacement or lost opportunity for someone else to become a tenant. Thirty-five years on, households for whom council housing previously provided a foot on the housing ladder have reduced access to housing. The Right to Buy has contributed to a substantial reduction of the social housing stock, and without replacement programmes, has reduced choice for existing and potential tenants.

Because the impact of the Right to Buy at estate level has also been uneven, and this has not generally been mitigated by regeneration and other investment activity, some estates have greater concentrations of households with problems, with higher incidences of crime and more victims of crime. The Right to Buy and policies to engineer tenure mix do not address the factors that generate concentrations of disadvantaged households in certain neighbourhoods. Without purposive actions to address underlying causes of neighbourhood decline or disadvantage, the Right to Buy and other housing and welfare policies may increase residential inequalities and divisions. Privatisation has also made the management of these neighbourhoods more complicated. Because of fragmented ownership and higher turnover of population, there is reduced capacity for social or management control. None of this represents a formula that would seem likely to have been appealing had it been set out in a manifesto or green paper.

The social housing that remains is more concentrated in cities, and flats form a higher proportion of properties. Many former council dwellings are now beyond the reach of households seeking to rent and previously able to do so in the council sector. In some cases these properties are available as private tenancies but attract higher rents that affect household budgets and ability to save. Rather than detaching government from housing, the Right to Buy left the government with greater subsidy (Housing Benefit) obligations for private tenants than they would have incurred for council tenants. At the same time, unanticipated problems related to Right to Buy leaseholds generated a succession of costly consultations and initiatives, and kept the government deeply involved in part of the privatised market. Some initiatives have financial implications and have protected Right to Buy leaseholders from the full financial consequences of their decision to buy. This was not the expectation in a privatisation programme designed to leave households to face the risks and opportunities afforded by private ownership.

6
THE NEXT PHASE: EXTENDING THE RIGHT TO BUY IN ENGLAND

Introduction

While the Right to Buy reduced the council housing stock, housing associations were sheltered from it and, from the mid-1980s, became the government's preferred vehicle for new rented housing. Housing associations also expanded rapidly through stock transfers stimulated by private finance and public policy, and by 2015 they provided more housing in England than local authorities. Very large housing associations have emerged with approaches to management, merger and business planning that reflected a belief in economies of scale. Some had lost the distinctiveness associated with their histories and where and why they initially operated. In 2015, however, there were proposals to extend the Right to Buy to housing associations in England.

Policy debates

In the lead-up to the 2015 general election there were a series of press stories about Conservative Party ideas for electorally attractive policies, and plans to further extend the Right to Buy in England. Conservative governments since the mid-1980s had favoured housing associations (rather than local authorities) as the vehicles to provide new rented housing, promote low cost home ownership and manage rented housing: private finance, regulation that gave comfort to private lenders and government grants supported the growth of housing associations. By 2015 however the leadership of the Conservative Party had moved away from this position and had become highly critical of housing associations. The origins of this shift in position are not entirely clear but seem to have been stimulated by contributions through the new generation of political think tanks seeking to influence government rather than objectively assess evidence. A paper jointly written by a Conservative and a Labour MP (Davis and Field, 2012) and published by the 'progressive' Institute for Public Policy Research, argued for the extension of the Right to Buy to housing association tenants and the reinvestment of capital receipts, This paper wrongly asserted that the collapse in the rate of sales under RTB after 2004 could be attributed to reductions in the average discount and to stock transfers. Another paper (Morton,2012) published by the Policy Exchange (supported by senior figures within the Conservative Party) presented an argument for the sale of high-value public housing to generate funds to invest in housing. The theme was taken up in another paper, published by the Policy Exchange (Walker, 2014). Walker emphasised issues of regulation, rents, disposal of stock and the use of balance sheet surpluses to invest in new housing and made the case for a radical change in the approach to housing associations. His arguments highlighted the ambitions of larger housing associations and made the case for changing arrangements to encourage associations to increase investment and respond to market opportunities. The general assertions about the housing association sector were in tune with the rhetoric subsequently associated with George Osborne and other Conservatives in the lead up to the general election of 2015.

These papers took little account of available research evidence and generally accepted an uncritical view of the Right to Buy. They asserted that restrictions on discounts introduced in 1999 explained the decline of Right to Buy, and they reflected the increasing anxiety at the failure of government policy to increase housebuilding. The opportunity to combine the popular appeal of the Right to Buy with increasing investment in housing required higher Right to Buy discounts, extending the policy to housing associations, selling high-value council properties, and committing to using the capital receipts generated by these sales to finance replacement housing.

The Right to Buy was no longer just about expanding home ownership, but was also linked to mechanisms that appealed economically and offered a way of addressing the crisis in housing and housing shortages. These proposals were worthy of examination, but there were unanswered (and unaddressed) questions about their feasibility and impacts, especially consequences for social and spatial segregation. In December 2013 Alex Morton became Prime Minister David Cameron's new planning and housing adviser, and his new role was reported to involve writing the planning and housing section of the Conservative Party's manifesto at the 2015 general election.

During the coalition government there was no formal consultation or evaluation of proposals to extend the Right to Buy to housing associations or of why policies to limit the Right to Buy in Scotland and Wales were inappropriate for England. There was for example no equivalent of the detailed and systematic analysis completed and published in Scotland (e.g. Scottish Executive 2006). In this context it is worth looking in more detail at the decision taken to abolish the Right to Buy in Scotland (Scottish Government, 2013). Ministers in Scotland had already removed the Right to Buy for new homes and new tenants in order to strengthen the social housing sector. While it had provided new options over the last 30 years, the costs of the policy would fall on future generations. A distinctive Scottish solution, meeting the needs of, and reflecting the values of, the people of Scotland emphasised that discounts of up to 70% for some tenants were unfair on other tenants, and on landlords who would lose an asset and not get enough money to replace it. Other reasons for abolition were the demand for social housing, with almost 400,000 people on waiting lists and high rates of application for homelessness assistance; the difficulties that Right to Buy created for existing tenants over rents and moving to homes more suited to their needs; helping social landlords to plan for the future and better manage their assets;

helping build sustainable communities with different housing tenures that people want to live in; preventing higher Housing Benefit costs associated with properties in the private rented sector; and removing unjustifiable and excessive discounts. The Right to Buy was extremely complex, and many tenants and landlords found it confusing and difficult to operate. Finally, the Scottish government would support people who aspired to home ownership through other initiatives that were better and more cost-effective than the Right to Buy and did not have a detrimental effect on the social rented sector.

Discussion of the Right to Buy in England involved assertion and exhortation but ignored most of the considerations referred to in Scotland. It was not open to evidence-based discussion. Proposals to embark on a new phase of the Right to Buy in England came from within the Conservative Party as part of its search for policies that would appeal to the electorate. They were not initially subject to sustained scrutiny, and perhaps were not taken very seriously as opinion polls suggested that it was very unlikely that the Conservatives would achieve sufficient support to form a government outright. Nevertheless, the Conservative manifesto included a commitment to 'extend the Right to Buy to tenants in Housing Associations to enable more people to buy a home of their own. It is unfair that they should miss out on a right enjoyed by tenants in local authority homes' (Conservative Party, 2015, p 52).

Clarke et al (2015) note that the Conservative Party press release that accompanied the manifesto launch stated that the government would fund the extension of the Right to Buy, allowing the replacement of stock bought by tenants with new affordable housing on a one-for-one basis. Local authority properties that ranked among the most expensive third of all properties (including private housing) of that type in their area would be sold off as they fell vacant, and replaced in the same area with normal affordable housing. This would involve the sale and replacement of around 15,000 homes a year. Although sold housing association properties would also be replaced on a one-for-one basis, the commitment fell short of replacement in the same area. Funds from the sale of high-value council properties were also to be invested in a Brownfield Regeneration Fund of £1 billion over five years.

The proposal to adopt a Right to Buy for housing associations raised the same issues as it had in 1980, but because many housing associations were now larger and substantially funded by the private sector, additional issues were involved. The business plans and asset management strategies adopted by housing associations and underpinning funding by the private sector were based on an established system of regulation and consents that gave funders confidence. The proposals related to the Right to Buy could destabilise strategies and damage the confidence of private financial institutions – representing a new risk that could affect performance and investment plans. These proposals were not initially welcomed by housing associations and were criticised by Shelter, the TUC, leading figures within housing associations and the NHF and by other political parties. During the election campaign, arguments related to independence, charitable aims and status, financing, investment and asset management strategies were presented as reasons to reject what was being proposed. In the tradition of the British tabloid press these arguments were countered with denunciations of the self-interest of over-paid housing association chief executives rather than engagement with the issues raised.

The outcome of the 2015 general election was a Conservative government able to command a majority in Parliament without support from other parties. Within two months of the election it became clear that the new government intended to pursue the extended Right to Buy policy set out in the Conservative manifesto. Housing associations would also have to adapt to changes in the government's approach to rents, and in September 2015, the Office for National Statistics (ONS) announced that it was to reconsider whether housing associations were properly regarded as part of the private sector. These changes had profound implications for their operation and future: while debate about the impact of Right to Buy continued, it increasingly took second place behind fundamental issues of the independence and financial viability of housing associations.

The government announced, in its first budget (8 July 2015), that the discretionary scheme introduced in 2012, to charge higher rents to higher-income social tenants, would become compulsory in England. In what would be referred to as 'Pay to Stay', social tenants with high incomes (£40,000 in London, £30,000 elsewhere) would, in future, be charged higher (market or near market) rents than other tenants. This, along with the proposed review of lifetime tenancies in social housing, with a view to limiting their use, would involve costs and implementation problems, but was broadly consistent with the coalition government's existing approach. Changes in policy towards rents, however, broke an established pattern.

Since the 1980s social rents had consistently been increased in real terms, annually (most recently at 1% above the rate of inflation) in order to narrow the gap between social and market rents. Under the new policy, rents (social and affordable) would fall in England by 1% a year for four years from April 2016 – achieving a 12% reduction in average rents by 2020/21. This would be introduced by the Welfare Reform and Work Bill and apply to housing associations and local authorities (although not where the Regulator determined that compliance would jeopardise a housing association's financial viability). This change highlighted how, by 2015, policies towards rents were being driven by a welfare agenda. Higher rents, in a sector with a high proportion of tenants in receipt of Housing Benefit, would involve higher Housing Benefit costs for the Exchequer. Lower rents reduced the social security bill and transferred the risk to social landlords. Limiting rent increases also reduced the impact of actions to reduce or freeze benefits, introduced at the same time.

The rent proposals came as a shock for housing associations whose business plans had been built on expectations of continuity in government policy. New approaches to rents and the Right to Buy changed the assumptions underpinning the operation and development plans of housing associations. Their reaction was that, as independent social businesses, they should not be mandated to charge specific rents. While a cut in rents over the next four years would be a real help for some tenants, it would have a negative impact on the development capacity of almost all housing associations. The Office for Budget Responsibility (OBR) had suggested that the rent reduction would lead to around 14,000 fewer affordable homes being built over the four-year period, but the National Housing Federation (NHF) estimated that there would be a loss of almost £3.85 billion in rental income over the four years, and at least 27,000 fewer new affordable homes would be built. For some housing associations changes could affect their agreements with lenders, the terms surrounding existing debt and ability to attract loan finance in the future.

Alongside these changes the Office for National Statistics (ONS) unexpectedly announced (September 2015) a review of the statistical classification of Private Registered Providers (PRPs) of social housing in England. This was the official term for housing associations registered with the Homes and Communities Agency (HCA); those not registered with the HCA, were outside of the scope of the review. A review of housing associations' status as public or private bodies raised the possibility that housing association borrowing could be reclassified as public debt. The ONS maintained that the review would be undertaken solely on the basis of current legislation, and in view of the legislative and regulatory changes brought about through the Housing and Regeneration Act 2008. It would establish whether PRPs should continue to be recorded as private non-financial corporations in ONS economic statistics, or should be changed, and would also ensure that the statistical treatment was consistent with the international guidance in the 2010 European System of Accounts. The ONS view was that this was simply about auditing government accounts, and the test applied was where control over the organisation lay. Housing associations feared that it could have more fundamental consequences for housing associations' capacity to borrow, their corporate strategy and day-to-day operation.

Housing associations were faced with three possible changes (Right to Buy, rents and reclassification as public bodies) that they disliked and that affected their independence. While they were unlikely to influence decisions on rents and benefits or whether or not housing associations were public bodies, the experience of 1980 suggested that opposition to Right to Buy proposals could be successful. Initially this seemed how the debate would develop, but the case made by the NHF against the proposals was met by hostile and sometimes distorted representations of housing associations' role and record.

In July 2015, for example, *Inside Housing* referred to articles published on the same day, in *The Spectator* and *The Times*. These criticised housing associations for not building enough homes but contained gross inaccuracies related to their history and origins, their record of building, and to grant support (Brown, 2015). The Chancellor of the Exchequer speaking to the House of Lords Economic Affairs Committee (8 September 2015) adopted the same theme. He castigated housing associations and stated that they faced a 'simple choice' on the Right to Buy extension: 'They can either work with us … or there can be a more confrontational relationship,….' He argued that, in contrast with public bodies and private companies, housing associations had not been under much pressure to be efficient in recent years and were not actively building enough homes. As evidence he stated 'four out of five housing associations built no properties last year.' This appeared to be a conscious exercise in misinformation. Most housing associations were charities receiving no government grant; and older associations had built or acquired much of their stock without government grant. Many associations' activities had for years been largely limited to managing dwellings. The statistics, rather than indicating failure, simply reflected the diversity of organisations operating as housing associations and the variety of responses to a changing market and policy environment. Indeed the pressures coming from successive governments and regulators since the late 1980s had increased the concentration of new building programmes in a small number of associations. Housing associations had been encouraged to access cheaper funds, take advantage of economies of scale and drive down costs. Mergers and group structures had been encouraged and funding was increasingly concentrated on the larger associations that adopted the preferred model. The disingenuous and confrontational tone of remarks was, however, an indicator of what could be expected if housing associations remained 'oppositional'.

A Voluntary Right to Buy

Rather than being oppositional, associations needed a compromise, on the Right to Buy and other matters. The risks for housing associations of a further deterioration of their relationship with the government and an escalation of hostilities were too great. Some associations were, in any case, comfortable selling properties as part of asset management strategies or where market values were achieved and their balance sheets were not compromised. For example, in 2012, the Chief Executive of Home Group, with 50,000 properties across England, Scotland and Wales, had identified major advantages in adopting a Right to Buy. This could move housing associations away from reliance on government grants and replacing sales on a one-for-one basis (see Wilson, 2014). For other (especially larger, expanding) housing associations the issues of independence and the risks associated with reclassification as public bodies made compromise imperative. Consequently the NHF worked with its members to put a collective offer to the government for housing associations to adopt a voluntary scheme that would replace existing proposals, avoid primary legislation setting the Right to Buy in stone, and avoid the government facing opposition in the House of Lords. This approach appeared to preserve the independence of housing associations, for which it represented the least worst option.

The proposal for a Voluntary Right to Buy drawn up by the NHF was announced by the Secretary of State, Greg Clark, at its conference in September 2015, and he set a very tight timetable for housing associations to decide whether or not to adopt it. The NHF recommended, to its members, an offer that had been prepared jointly with government. Housing associations would be fully compensated for the market value of the homes they sold. Although the NHF did not endorse the proposal to sell vacant high-value council-owned homes, it insisted that its offer depended on the government providing full funding for the discount, so that housing associations could replace the homes sold. The House of Commons Communities and Local Government Committee referred to the voluntary deal as including a commitment from the Government to review the regulatory burden on housing associations and reforming disposal and asset management regimes to smooth the delivery of the policy. It described the process as follows:

> 'In order to meet Parliamentary timelines and the publication of the Housing and Planning Bill, housing associations were given only a little over a week to tell the NHF whether or not they supported the voluntary agreement as an alternative to statutory enforcement of RTB. Inside Housing reported the outcome of the votes as 323 housing associations backing the proposals, 37 voting against, and 11 associations formally abstaining; 213 did not reply. The ballot was secret, and the NHF did not release details of how individual associations voted. However the NHF did announce that the 323 members who voted in favour of the voluntary agreement owned a total of 2.26m homes, which represented 93 per cent of the total housing association stock' (House of Commons, 2016a).

Although the NHF emphasised support for the voluntary scheme other commentaries highlighted the 45% of NHF members that did not back the deal, the lack of time to consult and the stage-management of the process by the NHF. While the 15 largest housing associations in London appear to have voted in favour of the proposal other smaller associations and those outside London were less united.in their approach and some of those that favoured the agreement had reservations and doubts (Zeffman, 2015).

On the same day that the result of the ballot was declared, the Prime Minister announced, at the Conservative Party conference, 'a historic new agreement with housing associations and the National Housing Federation that will extend the Right to Buy to 1.3 million more families across the country', and 'Some people said this would be impossible and that housing associations would never stand for it. Today we have secured a deal with housing associations to give their tenants the Right to Buy their home' (quoted in DCLG, 2015).

The NHF regarded agreement over the Voluntary Right to Buy as hugely important for the sector. It preserved boards' control over assets, protected the independence of the sector and ensured that associations were fully compensated for homes they sold and were able to replace every home sold. Beyond this, the agreement also marked a significant development in the relationship with the government, and paved the way for constructive discussions in the future. The first test of this came when the ONS announced its decision on the classification issue (30 October 2015). It concluded that housing associations that were PRPs were public market producers, and should be reclassified to the public non-financial corporations sub-sector in national accounts and other economic statistics. This classification applied from 22 July 2008, the date of enforcement of the Housing and Regeneration Act 2008. The reasons given for reclassification included the government's extensive consent powers including those related to disposals of housing stock, the use of disposal proceeds and powers over the management and appointment of managers and officers. Following this decision and consistent with the partnership established over Voluntary Right to Buy, the government made a commitment to bring in changes necessary to prompt the ONS to reverse the decision and take housing associations off the public balance sheet.

The next priority for the NHF was to ensure that the Right to Buy agreement worked for its members. The Voluntary Right to Buy meant that (subject to eligibility requirements) every housing association tenant would have the right to purchase a home at Right to Buy level discounts. The presumption was that housing associations would sell the tenant the property in which they lived. The government would compensate the housing association for the discount, and housing associations would retain the sales receipt to enable them to reinvest in new homes, with flexibility to replace rented homes with other tenures including shared ownership. There would be circumstances where a property could be excluded from sale (where it was in a very rural area or adapted for tenants with special needs). In these exceptional cases, housing associations would offer tenants the opportunity to use their discount to buy an alternative home from their own or another association's stock.

Having obtained agreement to the Voluntary Right to Buy it was now necessary to work on the detail of implementation. Individual housing associations were asked to consider how it would affect their business plans, to identify areas of risk and to address various detailed issues – how the replacement obligation would work, exemptions for rural areas and 'supported housing', the position of tenants in breach of tenancy agreements or with Anti-Social Behaviour Orders, properties in demolition programmes, the cost floor/outstanding debt calculation, alternatives to be offered to tenants whose property was excluded, where funds would come from to enable tenants to purchase on the open market and the annual cap on discounts. There were governance questions about how Voluntary Right to Buy and charity status would be resolved, how the HCA would approve disposals and about agreements with lenders. Other issues related to the disposal of properties transferred from local authorities with agreements, perhaps preventing resale and related to the prevention of fraud or abuse and up-front fees for tenants.

In effect, all of the issues previously encountered under the existing Right to Buy had to be revisited in the light of the different legal, financial and governance arrangements for housing associations and the 'voluntary' nature of the new scheme, with the implication that there was scope to negotiate an outcome that was more acceptable to housing associations.

Further policy development

Following the agreement on Voluntary Right to Buy, the Housing and Planning Bill 2015 and the Chancellor's Autumn Statement (November 2015) set out a housing policy to build 1 million new houses by 2020 and to significantly expand home ownership. The Help to Buy equity loan scheme was to be extended to 2021, and a London Help to Buy scheme introduced. Measures were announced to deliver 400,000 affordable housing starts by 2020/21, with a focus on low-cost home ownership and including £2.3 billion to help deliver 200,000 Starter Homes that could be sold to first-time buyers at 80% of market price. The commitment of £4 billion to build 135,000 new shared ownership homes by 2020/21 with higher levels of grant per home than previously and fewer restrictions on access was seen as an opportunity for housing associations. The plans for continued funding for social rented homes were much less ambitious, and it appeared that the last tranche of grant for social rented housing (rather than the higher rent affordable housing) was being allocated by the HCA for 2016/17.

These measures and the Voluntary Right to Buy were designed to ensure that home ownership would grow. The Right to Buy and Voluntary Right to Buy operating alongside reductions in investment in social rented housing and changes in rents would reduce the size of the social rented sector. If housing associations had colluded in a compromise agreement that protected themselves, they had failed to negotiate wider gains for the public and social rented sector as a whole, or for households whose best chance of obtaining good quality housing was in this sector.

As part of the spending review (25 November 2015), the government announced five Right to Buy pilots, selected by the government without consulting the NHF. Five housing associations operating in different markets in London, the South East, North West and East agreed to pilot the scheme to enable learning from their experience and preparation for the wider roll-out. In order to start the scheme, the Department for Communities and Local Government (DCLG) would initially finance discounts. Tenants living in the pilot areas could buy their own home immediately, with other tenants waiting until later in 2016, after the Housing and Planning Bill had received Royal Assent and the systems and processes for implementation had been worked through. At that stage, funds from the sale of high-value council properties would become available – with the DCLG managing the flow.

The NHF and DCLG set up an Implementation Advisory Board that would be supported by three further groups and meet regularly to ensure the system worked. The NHF would chair regular meetings of the Board until the Housing Bill received Royal Assent. It proposed the membership of this group, aiming to reflect the diversity of the sector, and made a direct link with the pilot schemes, through the involvement of Sovereign Housing, a large Oxfordshire housing association. While the DCLG, NHF and HCA were members of the Board, no reference was made to local government representation, although their interests were directly involved, and no reference was made to local housing strategies or combined authorities strategies to support economic and regeneration objectives. The dominant agendas for the government and independent housing associations appeared difficult to pursue in conjunction with other aspects of localism.

The Housing and Planning Bill, published on 13 October 2015, provided for most of the details of Right to Buy policies to be specified later by the Secretary of State through regulations. This included the definition of high-value dwellings. It set out, however, that the money from the sale of higher-value local authority dwellings would be charged to local authorities as a fixed sum, which they must pay – rather than handing over actual receipts from sales. The amount to be paid would be determined by estimating the value of high-value stock likely to become vacant during a year, and the details related to this would emerge later. The Bill stated that local authorities must consider selling any high-value stock becoming vacant, and must take account of any guidance given to them by the Secretary of State. The Bill provided for grants to be paid to housing associations to compensate them for selling homes at a discount.

Later government amendments (5 January 2016) to the Housing and Planning Bill were designed to prompt the ONS to reverse the reclassification decision and to take housing associations back off the public balance sheet. The amendments included removing the need for consent from the HCA for a variety of actions including tenanted and vacant stock disposals. To be consistent with the deregulation of the sector, Pay to Stay would also remain voluntary for housing associations.

Likely impact of Voluntary Right to Buy

The early steps taken over the Voluntary Right to Buy involved an incremental and pragmatic approach, in contrast with the introduction of the Right to Buy in 1980, when detailed regulation, distrust and centralised scrutiny were evident. Although it seems unlikely that the government will favour major departures from the Right to Buy template, the Voluntary Right to Buy may proceed in a different way with different qualifying periods and exemptions. The economic and housing context for Voluntary Right to Buy and levels of discount are all different than in 1980, and housing association property types, ages, values and locations do not match the council stock in 1980. In view of this it is difficult to provide a robust assessment of the likely impact of the scheme. Notwithstanding these differences it is salutary to remember the underestimation of the volume of sales completed under the Right to Buy in the period immediately after its introduction and subsequently. It would be wrong to assume a limited uptake of Voluntary Right to Buy among housing association tenants because a high proportion of them are elderly or economically inactive, and only just over a quarter of heads of household were working full-time. There is likely to be some pent-up demand because housing association tenants have been excluded from the Right to Buy, wish to continue to live in their home, and have the resources to buy.

Discounts make purchase attractive to households in less secure and well-paid jobs, and this may mean a relatively high proportion of buyers who will experience problems meeting housing costs – although not necessarily reaching the point where unplanned sale or repossession is involved. The willingness of banks and building societies to lend may prove critical, and the high levels of discount that reduce risk and make lending on Right to Buy attractive may not have the same effect if the requirements under Mortgage Conduct of Business rules exclude some tenants from purchasing. Low interest rates may make more tenants willing to take on a mortgage, but the availability of mortgages for 'marginal' purchasers has tightened considerably since the 1980s and 1990s.

The independent National Audit Office (2016), as part of its examination of whether government Departments have used their resources efficiently, effectively, and with economy provided a highly critical verdict on the government's evaluation of the new proposals for the RTB in England. It regarded the evaluation as weak and particularly criticised the failure to consider alternatives to meet the policy objectives, the failure to quantify and monetise costs and benefits and the failure to justify assumptions with evidence or sensitivity analysis. The National Audit Office report referred to experience from the reinvigorated RTB and the wider history of the RTB as suggesting that impacts over time could include a temporary (up to three or more years) reduction in council and housing association properties to rent, more conversion to private renting, a change in the geography of social rented housing and fewer properties available for social renting in the longer term as replacement homes are at higher affordable rents.

The Voluntary Right to Buy may involve more exemptions of properties than under the Right to Buy, and the possibility exists of offering tenants exercising the Voluntary Right to Buy the opportunity to buy elsewhere. If these mechanisms are widely used, the impacts of policy will be different, but because they will inevitably be more complex and involve different procedures, there will be issues of clarity and cost and a greater potential for conflict. Consequently they may only be used in exceptional cases, and patterns of Voluntary Right to Buy sale are likely to be similar to those experienced under the Right to Buy:

- An uneven geography of sales is likely and will have implications for how discounts and replacements are financed. The discounts for housing association sales completed in districts that have no council stock will, in effect, be funded by the sale of high-value housing owned by other local authorities.
- Subject to eventual exemptions, housing associations are likely to sell more of their better properties in better locations. The (unintended) consequence will be to change the mix of properties they own (more flats and one-bedroom properties), and to change their

geography. Housing associations may as a consequence be less able to respond appropriately to the needs of new and existing tenants.

- Sales are likely to be higher among houses with gardens and among longer established tenants entitled to higher discounts and at the stage in the family cycle where they are most likely to be able to buy.
- Unless exemptions are more effective than under Right to Buy, the loss of some dwellings that are a resource for households with mobility problems or with disabilities, and of dwellings in rural and other areas with very limited stocks of social rented housing, will be sold – this will affect local capacity to respond to demand from households with special needs and strong links to places.
- Sales of flats may be high in some areas partly because this will make moving home in the future easier, and this may indicate more rapid resale of these properties with consequent implications for management.
- Sales are likely to be lowest in recently built properties if historic cost considerations apply.

New issues related to leasehold management are unlikely to arise, and some housing associations already have experienced, professional leasehold management teams. Others will need to invest in training and the development of procedures. However, purchasers of dwellings of non-traditional construction are entitled to some reassurance about the willingness of lenders to provide mortgages for future sale of the property. It is likely that some housing association tenants will undertake purchases with family members who could subsequently put pressure on the purchaser to move. There is also a strong likelihood of third party speculative involvement, and it is unclear what measures to prevent abuse of Voluntary Right to Buy will be applied, and whether high discounts increase the risks of abuse. Although measures to address abuse had been introduced it seems unlikely that they were wholly effective and in 2015 the London Borough's Fraud Investigators' Group reported that fraud cases had more than doubled in the previous year and that at least 3% of RTB applications were fraudulent – raising concerns that some tenants were being exploited by people wanting to take advantage of the opportunities provided by increased discounts (House of Commons, 2016a, p.16).

The issues referred to above are largely immediate issues of the management and impact of the Voluntary Right to Buy, but the discussion in this book has emphasised serial failures to consider long-term policy consequences. In this respect, the strategic challenges faced by the Voluntary Right to Buy will not all be addressed by adjustments to the scheme itself or by individual housing associations. They require consideration of how the whole housing system adjusts to changes in tenure and access at a sub-regional and local level, and how replacement by housing associations and local authorities is coordinated and contributes to meeting local needs and local strategies. There are issues related to access to housing among lower-income groups, vulnerable households and people with needs for particular types of housing and support or for housing in rural areas. Other issues arise over how Voluntary Right to Buy and exemptions affect plans for the regeneration of estates and investment strategies associated with the redesign and renewal of estates. Especially where sales involve older properties and low-income households, the condition of the sold stock may also be a long-term concern in some areas.

Voluntary Right to Buy sales and replacement

Although some critical details of Voluntary Right to Buy may remain unclear until the experience of pilots can be assimilated, estimates of its potential impact were made at an early stage, and the most substantial of these (Clarke et al, 2015; Perry et al, 2015) referred to other analysis.

Voluntary Right to Buy sales by housing associations

The two early estimates of how many properties would be sold under Voluntary Right to Buy were from the NHF and Savills. The NHF suggested that 850,000 housing association tenants could be eligible, and just under a quarter might be able to afford a mortgage, generating some 220,000 sales over five years; Savills estimated that around

377,000 housing association tenants, or 20%, would be able to afford to buy their home, and that 24,000 per annum would do so. A later estimate (Perry et al, 2015), that about 1.45 million housing association tenants would be eligible, judged that tight mortgage market rules would mean that only about 10% of this group (145,000) would buy in the first five years. Finally, Clarke et al (2015) estimated that 970,000 housing association tenants would qualify for the Voluntary Right to Buy, but only 185,000 would be able to afford to exercise it, and 128,000 would exercise the right in the first five years.

These sources present wildly different estimates – from 120,000 to 220,000. The experience of the Right to Buy some 35 years ago does, however, suggest that some purchasers are drawn from households that researchers have determined cannot afford to buy. The capacity to access loans from within the family or other sources, beyond the limits suggested by researchers, may provide grounds to expect higher sales than suggested in the lowest estimates.

The estimates of the volume of sales provide a basis for assessing the costs of discounts for Voluntary Right to Buy sales, the volume of local authority sales needed to fund discounts and the scale of replacement housing needed.

High-value local authority sales

The initial issue arising from the compulsory sale of high-value local authority housing to finance the Voluntary Right to Buy scheme is how many council dwellings will be sold. Discounts associated with Voluntary Right to Buy can reasonably be assumed to be similar to the average discount of £60,000 associated with the existing Right to Buy (see Table 4.4 in Chapter Four). At 30,000 sales a year, the annual cost of discounts would be £1.8 billion – £9 billion over five years. This would be the charge local authorities would be required to pay to fund discounts, and the charges would be set by government based on estimates of the numbers of high-value properties they have and that become vacant.

Government indications are that around 15,000 higher-value council homes would be expected to be sold each year to enable local authorities to recover the annual charge imposed on them (Clarke et al, 2015). The framework for the policy is assumed to be similar to proposals made by the Policy Exchange and Conservative Party press releases (quoted in Perry et al, 2015). These involve setting regional house price thresholds for different types and sizes of property and based on the values of the top third of all dwellings in all tenures in each category. Local authority dwellings with open market values above the threshold will be sold on the market when they become vacant.

Clarke et al (2015) identify regional thresholds for different property types and sizes, and estimate the flow of vacant properties, based on rates of tenancy turnover of local authority stock in each category. They estimate that in England some 106,000 local authority dwellings become vacant each year, with just over 12,000 in the high-value categories. Unless the threshold for high value is set lower, there will not be 15,000 sales a year, and local authorities will be unable to make payments that assume this level of sales. Either other budgets at central or local level will be drawn on, or the whole scheme will operate with lower thresholds. This problem becomes more acute year on year. As higher-value stock is sold, the higher-value stock from which sales can take place diminishes.

The commitment to housing associations to refund discounts can be assumed to be the first call on the proceeds from completed local authority sales. This amounts (from above) to £1.8 billion a year, which is the equivalent of £150,000 each for the 12,000 high-value sales estimated to be forthcoming by Clarke et al (2015). Because the scheme will operate at a regional level, the amounts needed to repay discounts will be lower where sales values are lower, but it is expected that repayment of discount to be well within reach everywhere. In London and the South East the target of replacing every high-value sale with two properties (in addition to the housing association replacement) is likely to prove possible and has made the scheme more acceptable, although questions about location and type of replacement remain. Elsewhere the highest value properties may only generate sufficient receipts to enable a lower cost replacement that may not match what is needed locally.

Although thresholds are set regionally, there are likely to be much higher proportions of local authority stock sold in the East Midlands, East of England and London than elsewhere (Clarke et al, 2015). Some types of properties are also much more likely to be sold. If the high-value sales definition embraces all properties, the immediate loss of relets in some areas and parts of the council stock may create chronic shortages of certain types of property, including supported and sheltered housing and bungalows.

It is important at this stage to note that by 2015 almost one in every two local authorities in England no longer had any significant council housing. Most shire districts had transferred their stock to housing associations, while London boroughs and metropolitan districts were most likely to still be landlords and had the largest dwelling stocks. Housing associations generally had the largest share of the housing stock where local authorities had the smallest share. The mechanism for financing the sale of housing association dwellings consequently involves the transfer of resources within a region from areas with council housing to areas without.

Clarke et al (2015) calculate that there are 18 stock-owning local authorities without any high-value stock, and a further 41 with under 5% of their stock being high value. In some local authorities with high proportions of their council stock falling within the regional high-value threshold, a large proportion of the housing that would otherwise become available for letting will be sold off. In some cases less than half the properties becoming vacant will be relet. As the proportion of council stock left that is high value will be reduced through this policy, there are increasing problems over time. Even if the thresholds remain in line with house prices, the numbers of sales will gradually fall because of the changing composition of the sector after sales. Within a relatively short time local authorities' housing stock will not include any significant part of high-value properties in the top 30% value group, and this has implications for the geographical distribution of council housing. In effect, there is a forced relocation of council stock away from high-value areas.

Replacement

The financing of replacement housing involves drawing on receipts from the previous sale only to the extent needed to supplement borrowing against the rental income stream generated by the new property. The higher the rental income stream, the lower the cash supplement needed. Housing associations receiving the full market value of the dwelling sold and repaying any outstanding debt and other charges associated with the property and its sale will generally have more than sufficient funds to replace dwellings – especially in London. The critical decisions for them will be about the nature of replacement in terms of size, type, location, quality and tenure.

For local authorities to replace sold dwellings, they must have sufficient funds to finance new building and capacity to borrow against the rental income stream. The latter depends on central government rules related to prudential borrowing, and it cannot be assumed that these will facilitate replacement building in all cases. There is also a question over whether the funds remaining from high-value sale, once the charge levied by central government has been paid, is sufficient to fund new building – or whether the rate of vacancies occurring in the high-value stock and the receipts generated are insufficient to meet all the demands placed on them. The more Voluntary Right to Buy sales occur, the more local authorities will be charged by central government. The mechanism may prove insufficient, even if all high-value properties are sold when they become vacant, and this would eliminate any local strategic input to protect housing resources for local needs. In the event of high Voluntary Right to Buy sales, the proceeds from sales of high-value council homes may do little more than protect housing association balance sheets.

The final element in the policy involves what is meant by replacement, and how far replacement offsets the consequences for housing access of Voluntary Right to Buy and sales of high-value council housing. From the government's perspective, replacement goals are met by building properties that are to be for social or affordable rent, equity sharing or outright sale – no doubt evaluation will focus on numbers irrespective of type. But from a wider housing access and policy perspective, rent and tenure details, as well as size, type and location, are critical if replacements are to provide accessible and appropriate housing that matches local needs. Replacement housing could meet or exceed the target in terms of numbers but fail to be in the right place, of the right size and affordable for those in housing need. Clarke et al (2015) suggest that replacement of Voluntary Right to Buy sales will generate gains more quickly because each replacement dwelling provides a new housing opportunity while the loss of relets is only that proportion of sold properties (perhaps 4%) that would have become available for letting. In contrast, all of the high-value local authority sales represent an immediate loss of dwellings to the lettings pool: delays or failures to replace like with like affect local access and opportunity. They concluded that if social housing replaced stock, there would eventually be a positive impact on the availability of low-cost housing and on poverty. However, if houses are replaced with affordable rent homes, both poverty and Housing Benefit costs will rise, and if they are replaced with shared ownership or 'Starter Homes', these will be out of the reach of those that would access social housing. This would push more people into the private rented sector, further increasing both poverty and Housing Benefit costs.

The final issue about replacement relates to timing. The losses to social renting associated with both housing association and local authority sale of vacant dwellings can commence as soon as necessary legislation and other details are in place. There is an immediate impact on balance sheets as rental income is reduced – permanently or at least until replacement dwellings are provided. But land assembly, design, planning and procurement of replacement dwellings is likely to take three or more years. There is consequently a period in which the policy reduces the flow of vacancies of social rented housing and will add to homelessness and waiting times for rehousing. As with other effects, this will be particularly severe where local authorities own high-value stock.

Alternative scenarios

The policy puts the government in a strong position to achieve its goals, especially if they are expressed simply in terms of numbers. It also protects housing associations from the worst financial outcomes: sales generate capital receipts, discount payments are covered by government funding and overall receipts match market values and are generally sufficient to enable replacement. This, however, involves unplanned restructuring of assets rather than strategic asset management, and may pose challenges for smaller housing associations that have no development programme or staff. These associations could commission services from elsewhere but are forced into new territory and activity that their boards have not chosen. It may also pose substantial challenges for housing associations that have long-term commitments to popular neighbourhoods where they will be exposed to high rates of sale and there is no scope for new housing development.

While some housing associations will be content to switch away from social renting to other forms of provision, others will regard this as inconsistent with their aims and objectives and undesirable. The Voluntary Right to Buy may have already exposed different priorities and attitudes in the housing association sector – differences expressed by concerns about the process of negotiation with government, the timescale for consideration of the Voluntary Right to Buy offer and the weighting of votes in the ballot in favour of larger associations. In the subsequent stage, as Voluntary Right to Buy is implemented, housing associations are likely to react and change in different ways. One possibility is that housing associations will converge on a common model of professional property management without the wider social and economic ambitions associated with their histories, aims and objectives.

But it is local authorities that are most exposed by the policy. They are obliged to sell vacant units rather than let them to households in need, and they are likely to be obliged to change their dwelling stock in a way unrelated to patterns of need and demand. The residual council stock after five or ten years of high-value sales will have a different profile in terms of location, dwelling size, type and age. Local authorities will have lost control of key decisions that enable an effective response to tenants needing transfers and exchanges. The overall development of policy in England risks weakening the alternatives to market providers, and underestimates the contribution of housing associations and local authorities, working with and alongside the private sector to address housing problems and devise strategies that take account of local circumstances and needs.

Although it is not possible to provide a firm estimate of the impact of the Voluntary Right to Buy in England, it is possible to set out some alternative scenarios. These all operate against the background of wider housing policy, including the operation of the Right to Buy and its continuing (even if limited) impact on the council sector. Four possible scenarios serve to focus policy debate:

- There is little change because the Voluntary Right to Buy scheme proves to have limited appeal, or its detailed implementation proves problematic, and the steps taken to resolve difficulties prove problematic for buyers or sellers, or both. The Voluntary Right to Buy is taken up by small numbers of housing association tenants (with an uneven pattern in relation to properties and places). Its impacts, and those of other changes, are largely absorbed: business plans and strategies are essentially unchanged. The pressures on council disposals to finance discounts are important and affect the flow of relets, but to a limited extent because of the low rate of sales. The overall consequences for housing supply and access are limited, although the types of properties becoming available for letting and their locations change.
- The take-up of Voluntary Right to Buy is more substantial, but there are no significant problems of implementation or financing housing association replacements. Although significant numbers of housing association tenants buy and the pattern of sales is uneven,

business plans are able to be adjusted to deal with changes, and strategies are essentially unchanged. The tenants buying mainly remain in their properties, and turnover following sale is low. The impacts of these or other changes are largely absorbed by the housing association sector, but the pressures on council disposals to finance discounts are important and, because of the rate of sales and level of discounts, significantly affect the flow of relets. The consequences for housing supply and access (and replacement building by local authorities) is significant in some localities with high-value council stock. It affects the volume of council relets, the types of properties becoming available for letting and their locations: there is increasing homelessness and waiting times, less capacity to match lettings to needs, and a more concentrated geographical pattern of social lettings.

- The response to Voluntary Right to Buy is much more substantial, and along with changes affecting rents, has a widely disruptive effect. This includes a short-term impact on finances and business plans, leading to significant reductions in social housing supply, with replacement by housing associations largely consisting of affordable rent, shared equity and Starter Homes. The tenants buying under Voluntary Right to Buy include many who sell and move, and turnover following sale is relatively high and adds to management problems. There is a considerable transfer of properties to private renting, and this increases the costs to the Exchequer associated with Housing Benefit. Replacement also proves problematic for various reasons, including issues of funding, timing and site assembly. The pressure on council disposals to fund discounts is significant and affects the volume and location of relets sufficiently to create severe shortages in some property types and sizes and some locations. There are major consequences for housing supply and access, with the flow of relets in some parts of the council and housing association stocks drying up, with a measurable impact on households in housing need, the waiting times faced by potential tenants and on homelessness.
- Housing associations in different parts of the country and operating in different markets adopt very different strategies, either in

anticipation of the impacts of changes or because of them. Some conclude that their business will be strengthened if they cease to provide new social lettings and move to providing housing at market or near market rents. Others adopt more mixed strategies or cease to be active developing associations. The pressures on council disposals to fund discounts and the change from social to other lettings with higher rents affects the flow of relets and waiting times for social housing and has an impact on homelessness. The reduction in the supply of dwellings let at social or below market rent levels declines, and a significant proportion of properties sold under Voluntary Right to Buy become privately rented. With more of the households qualifying for Housing Benefit being in the higher rented private rented sector, there are significant consequences for Housing Benefit costs and household budgets, especially of lower-income and vulnerable households. There are major consequences for housing supply and access, with the flow of relets in some parts of the council and housing association stocks drying up.

Conclusions

For much of the period since 1980, a common Right to Buy policy had different consequences in different places across the UK, but more recently, policy in England, Scotland, Wales and Northern Ireland has diverged. The measures introduced in 2012 to reinvigorate the Right to Buy in England and the adoption of a Voluntary Right to Buy for housing association tenants will increase UK differences in housing tenure and access in the future. Although the Right to Buy has been restricted or abolished in Scotland and Wales, the intention in England is to increase its reach. The Voluntary Right to Buy in England involved an extravagant policy commitment, entered into during an election, with limited consideration of the implications for housing in different parts of the country, little informed debate, and limited preparation in terms of design, viability or financing. Any assumption that this was a simple extension of Right to Buy was naive. The different legal and financial status of housing associations meant that the policy had to be redesigned. The long list of only partly resolved issues of principle and implementation are evidence that the policy commitment fell far short of a workable template. The disruption to housing associations and their investment plans arising from this commitment and changes to policy affecting rents is likely to have adverse impacts on housebuilding, at least in the short term. In the longer term, even the most optimistic view suggests that increased problems of housing access will arise in some places.

The scheme devised for England aspires to increase housing supply by using funds released from sales of existing properties, with no overt demands placed on public expenditure. The commitment to replacement investment represented an acknowledgement that Right to Buy has consequences that demand new investment in affordable housing. The government can exploit the one-for-one replacement formula if the focus is simply on numbers, but the formula does not safeguard against increasing local shortages of social rented housing, leaving more low-income households dependent on insecure and expensive private renting and the government more exposed to high Housing Benefit costs.

The sale of local authority stock was to take place with no assessment of the consequences for local authorities' capacity to meet their duties in relation to housing and homelessness. Local authorities appear to have been left out of the negotiation over the Voluntary Right to Buy, and to have been shifted to the margins of the debate about housing. The rationale for financing discounts for housing association tenants through the forced disposal of high-value council stock works against policies to maximise the supply of lower-rent social rented housing and to improve asset management, choice and mix in the public sector. It involves a planned but locationally random dismantling of the remnant council housing sector.

For the government to grant very large discounts to enable well-housed households to buy their house and to fund this, to require local authorities to sell a property rather than let it, when there are homeless households and others waiting for such housing, raises questions not only of priorities and extravagance, but also of probity. There also appears to be an unspoken view that social housing should not be in high-value areas. Acting on such a view is likely to contribute to increasing social and spatial segregation and stigmatisation of social housing – enabling further denigration and demonisation of social housing and damaging to life chances.

There remain serious doubts about whether the Voluntary Right to Buy will work in volume terms or in providing the housing that is needed, where it is needed. The loss of relets occasioned by the sale of high-value council dwellings exposes the limitations of the commitment to replacement. At best, replacements are likely to be completed three years after vacant dwellings were taken from the lettings pool. At worst, replacements will not be accessible to households excluded by the decision to sell vacant council properties.

The arrangements for replacement of sold housing association properties and the council dwellings sold to fund this could address strategic housing issues associated with the loss of relets, but seems unlikely to stem the decline of social renting or its increased geographical concentration. There is no ambition in the policy agenda to have a good quality cost rent sector that competes with the private sector. The emphasis is on increasing owner-occupation especially through Help to Buy and Starter Homes, but even these schemes are unaffordable for households in poverty and for those whose incomes fluctuate. For these households, good quality, affordable social rented housing provides the best platform for the future.

There are concerns about the use of funds, generated by reducing the supply of council housing in one area, to finance extraordinary levels of discount to enable the growth of home ownership elsewhere. The situation is uncomfortably reminiscent of earlier scandals associated with selling empty property to prevent homeless households moving into areas in Westminster. Rather than being an ingenious scheme to fund the Voluntary Right to Buy, the sale of vacant properties involves a direct choice to delay housing homeless or other households in need in order to enable a well-housed family to buy. The trade-off has little about fairness or financial prudence or carrying out housing duties. The issue is made more contentious because of the possible scale of

Voluntary Right to Buy. In some places this could necessitate the sale of most of the high-value properties coming vacant – with a dramatic impact on the overall flow and mix of properties available to let. Some limits to the sale of vacant stock might moderate this effect, but the anomalies created suggest that the funding mechanism is inappropriate. The Treasury should fund Voluntary Right to Buy directly, or should provide pump-priming funding to ensure any loss of social housing lettings is replaced from the outset, and to meet costs if they are greater than a modest level. In addition, replacement targets should ensure a continuing growth in good quality social rented housing appropriate for local needs.

When introduced in the 1980s, the Right to Buy had a positive short-term impact on national accounts – it generated capital receipts rather than incurring public expenditure. The Treasury, unconcerned to invest these receipts in housing, received a windfall that helped balance its books and fund other expenditures. In the event, the failure to maintain the size of the social rented sector and the growth of private renting has left the Treasury with a self-inflicted continuing additional benefit cost. The costs of assistance with housing costs is greater if households entitled to benefit are paying private sector rents rather than lower social rents – the short-term gain has translated into a long-term exposure to higher expenditure.

As the debate about extending the Right to Buy in England developed, the focus shifted to the future and independence of housing associations. One view is that by caving in to the government and some larger housing associations, the NHF ended the debate about extending the Right to Buy before it began. Issues should have been closely examined in Parliament and problems identified at the outset rather than waiting until they arise. A less than open deal, between the government and powerful, wealthy housing associations, failed to take full account of all of the issues and interests involved. There was no open consideration of the issues considered in Scotland or Wales, and no opportunity to debate whether the same policy was appropriate for all cities and regions in England. There has been a dramatic switch in England from an approach, before 1979, when local authorities were empowered to make decisions on council house sales and housing needs to one in which central government decides without reference to local considerations or uneven impacts.

In April 2016 the House of Commons Committee of Public Accounts (House of Commons, 2016b) commented on the failure of the Government to publish a detailed impact assessment of the policy and the vagueness of assurances about how it would be funded. It also expressed concerns about the extent to which new homes funded by the policy would be genuine replacements and about controls to prevent abuses. Reservations continued to be expressed elsewhere about the legitimacy of forcing charitable housing associations to dispose of properties where this would compromise the legacy and strategy for which these associations were responsible. The case for exempting properties (especially those built without government grants) continued to be made and was particularly important for some of the oldest and best known charitable associations. The amendments to legislation that had been passed in the House of Lords, were not carried forward to the Housing and Planning Act 2016 which received Royal Assent on May 12th. However it could be some years before it was clear whether critical comments, from the Communities and Local Government Select Committee, the National Audit Office, the Committee of Public Accounts and others, about financing, implementation, replacement and impact, would prove justified. How the extended Right to Buy would operate in practice remained uncertain.

Housing associations in England considered themselves successful in having seen off a longstanding challenge to their independence. The 'deal' with government would give wide scope for boards to make decisions on rents, asset management, disposals and other matters. However, the rhetoric of independence may obscure other layers of regulation, control and culture. If housing associations have shaken off the chains of government control, whom do they remain accountable to, and what do they see as their distinctive role? Are their boards likely to adopt policies that are in the interests of tenants or households in housing need, or are these issues largely invisible to larger organisations whose boards have little or no direct representation of these groups, and are dominated by financial and property professionals, accountants and lawyers? Is their residual instinct to engage with problems faced by vulnerable households, to address neighbourhood problems, problems of urban renewal and the lack of access to housing faced by particular types of household – perhaps as their very differently constituted boards aspired to in the 1960s and 1970s? Or are they increasingly likely to operate as 'responsible' private landlords, maximising rent income and doing well what is required by law, but little more?

7
CONCLUSIONS: PUBLIC AND SOCIAL HOUSING: SLOW DEATH OR NEW BEGINNINGS?

Introduction

The Right to Buy marked a significant change of approach to housing in the UK. It was followed by a period in which the role of councils in shaping local housing declined along with council housing. After 35 years, it is now possible to offer a verdict on the success of the Right to Buy experiment. The policy rewarded one generation of tenants, and made a real difference for most of these households. Some 2 million Right to Buy sales between 1980 and 2015 increased the level of home ownership. While this could be seen as evidence of success, the incentives associated with the policy and the context in which it operated meant it would have been surprising had this not been achieved. A longer-term evaluation would refer to the failure to sustain home ownership at a higher level – the Right to Buy expanded home ownership temporarily through extraordinary discounts that were only available once for each property, and a significant proportion of these properties were transferred to other tenures on resale.

Without measures to reinvest the capital receipts from Right to Buy sales, housing shortages had also become a major concern across the

UK by 2016. New construction remained much lower than before 1980, and fell far short of what was needed to meet demographic change, let alone rising aspirations. There was growing evidence of unhealthy and inappropriate housing, alongside inflation of house prices at the top of the market. The Right to Buy forms part of the explanation for more severe housing problems, and the common reference to a housing crisis. From strategic and long-term perspectives the overall policy approach of successive governments has been a failure. There has been too little building, too little social housing to meet need or demand, too little local capacity to address problems of access, affordability and housing need, and too little attention given to the poor quality of much of the existing housing stock.

The government has faced increasing Housing Benefit costs associated with tenants paying market rents in the private sector – because there is too little public and social housing available with lower rents. In the absence of a strategy to rebuild public and social rented housing supply, public expenditure on Housing Benefit is likely to increase further, without generating the levels of investment in the housing stock that were achieved from spending on council housing. Local authorities have insufficient housing to meet the demands from homeless and vulnerable households, and they export problems to the insecure and expensive private rented sector and to local authorities elsewhere. While this can disrupt families and communities and fail to meet needs successfully, the costs involved for government are higher than they would have been if there was more social rented housing. Large numbers of households unable to meet market costs for housing are now in the growing private rented sector, and the costs to the public purse are greater than they would have been had they been housed in social rented housing.

Housing problems have increased since the Right to Buy, and are directly linked to the reduction in the size of the public and social rented sector, and the failure to reinvest the receipts from the sale of council houses in housing. It is undeniable that the Right to Buy could have been implemented alongside an investment programme designed to neutralise its adverse effects, but this path was not chosen.

The Right to Buy in retrospect and without any accompanying strategy for housing access and supply represents a failure in strategic thinking. It has left a legacy of housing shortage and increasing housing need, high subsidy to private sector housing and housing inequality. Its strategic implications are also associated with its effect on the supply of housing for older people and people with disabilities and the supply of housing in rural and other areas where there was only a small council and social housing stock. Measures designed to prevent the sale of purpose-built properties for older people or people with disabilities were put in place and had some impact, but other properties normally let to (but not purpose-built for) such groups were not excluded. In rural areas the loss of stock has been as rapid or more so, and planning-related measures and conditions restricting resale to locals have largely proved ineffective. In practice, the protection of the supply of housing for locals has relied on the activity of housing associations, and added to the attraction of stock transfer with its effect in limiting the Right to Buy to existing tenants (until the new measures agreed in 2015).

The Right to Buy?

The Right to Buy was introduced in 1980 following a period of sustained progress in housing. The 60 years between 1919 and 1979 saw the substantial growth of public sector housing, and by the late 1970s, some one in three dwellings in the UK were owned by local authorities or new towns. By international standards the state controlled a large sector. Most public sector housing was purpose-built family housing, equipped with modern amenities and built to high standards. It was better housing than was available in the private rented sector and much of the home ownership sector. It was housing that had been sought by affluent, employed households, and until the 1960s, had largely been beyond the reach of the poorest households. It is because of the size of the public sector housing stock, controlled principally by local authorities, and its quality and desirability that the Right to Buy was so attractive and important.

The Right to Buy was part of a policy approach that broke the long established pattern of support for an expanding council housing sector providing good quality housing at rents designed to cover costs and below market levels. It was, and continued to be, regarded as a vote winner, and was introduced as part of wider privatisation of housing provision. The approach was an experiment in much the same way that policies introducing subsidies for council housing had been 60 years earlier. With both experiments there were uncertainties about how the market would respond. In 1980, there was a belief that private activity had been crowded out by the state but would increase if councils reduced their activity. These beliefs were based on theory, ideology or dogma rather than evidence, and overlooked the historical failure of the market that had led previous governments to look to councils to play a major role. The risk was that reducing council provision and procurement would reduce supply and standards and widen housing inequality. The same policy experiment would also be unlikely to have the same impact everywhere – irrespective of local tenure structures, levels of demand and prices. The reduction in local ownership and control could weaken local procurement that had kept supply and standards high when private sector actors were inactive or preoccupied with catering for particular types of demand.

The immediate take-up of the Right to Buy in 1980-81 and the levels of sales in later years exceeded expectations, and the volume of sales was generally presented as establishing the policy as a success. Politicians continued to see the policy as an electoral asset, and consistently revived the policy as a vote winner. It generated greater immediate and continuing capital receipts than anticipated, but these were not reinvested in housing. The private sector did not increase its activities to fill the gap left by reduced council investment. Cautions expressed about the longer-term impacts of the policy – the loss of relets, housing access, segregation, the management of neighbourhoods or shortages of council housing and concerns about residualisation – were disregarded. The case for reinvestment of some or all of the capital receipts from Right to Buy sales in housing was largely ignored before 1997.

7. CONCLUSIONS

The Right to Buy undoubtedly proved a success for most purchasers. They bought assets at well below market values and were able to re-schedule their housing costs and secure their housing situation. Where the houses they bought appreciated in value, it represented a much more substantial asset than the entitlements associated with their tenancy, and it increased their ability to move house. Even where the property was less attractive or valuable, it opened different options than their council tenancy had. But the fact that the policy proved a success for most purchasers is not a sufficient argument for its extended operation, or for higher discounts to maintain sales, or for failing to consider whether the policy, in a changing context, involved adverse consequences for housing or public expenditure. The policy was reviewed in Scotland and Wales, but there was no overall evaluation or stocktake in England over 35 years: the focus on value for money in 1997/98 was more limited.

The transfer of over 2 million dwellings from the public sector to home ownership and subsequent sale of what is likely to prove in excess of 40% of these to private renting has changed each of these tenures. There is more low-cost home ownership, and it is in estates and neighbourhoods that previously had few or no homeowners. There are more low-income homeowners, and they have various levels of satisfaction with the tenure. Home ownership has not been a panacea, and dissatisfaction is almost as great among homeowners in lower Council Tax band properties as among council tenants in such properties. Council estates that are difficult to live in and to manage and have high concentrations of disadvantaged households have not been transformed through Right to Buy sales, and further sales are equally unlikely to change this. Indeed, the growth of private renting with fragmented ownership and variations in the quality of management and maintenance may add to problems.

Thirty-five years of the Right to Buy has reduced the housing that is accessible to households for whom council housing provided a foot on the housing ladder, and has reduced choice for existing and potential tenants. It has contributed to a substantial reduction of the social housing stock, and without countervailing new build programmes, has caused supply problems. Because the impact of the Right to Buy at estate level has also been uneven and this has not generally been mitigated by regeneration and other investment activity, some estates have greater concentrations of households with problems, with higher incidences of crime and victims of crime. Fragmented ownership and higher turnover of population has reduced capacity for social or management control, and made the management of council-built neighbourhoods more complicated. The social housing that remains is more concentrated in larger towns and cities, and flats form a higher proportion of properties.

Future prospects

Different parts of the UK have developed different approaches to housing policy. Devolution enabled Scotland, Wales and Northern Ireland to take different paths from England, and decisions were taken to abolish the Right to Buy in Scotland and Wales. If these policies remain in place, they will limit future impacts and increase the differences in housing between them and England. The overriding reason for the restriction (and then abolition) of the Right to Buy in Scotland and Wales was that, with the low rate of new additions to social housing, it was desirable to protect the existing supply of social housing from sale. By retaining public and social housing they will have a more mixed economy of housing, with different agencies procuring new construction and providing and managing housing. A less complete reliance on private sector providers suggests a pattern of new building that is planned and less affected by economic upturns and downturns, and a better, more even quality of management and maintenance. In these parts of the UK, public and social rented housing is regarded as a valuable asset, increasing the capacity to respond to economic as well as social problems.

In contrast, the approach to housing in England seems to involve a stronger reliance on the private sector, and a determination to reduce and weaken other housing providers. Local authorities' role in particular appears not to be valued, and policy actively sets out to dismantle the legacy of council housing and its future capacity. Neither the coalition government nor its Conservative successor has paid attention to the accumulated evidence about the Right to Buy or its value for money or the arguments being advanced in other parts of the UK. The level and reach of incentives associated with the Right to Buy were increased, although the logic of the rest of the government's approach to housing and public expenditure might have suggested reductions and different priorities. In England the extended Right to Buy of 2012 and the Voluntary Right to Buy of 2015 leave the public and social rented housing sectors likely to continue to decline. The disruption to housing associations and their investment plans arising from the Voluntary Right to Buy and changes affecting rents in the social sector is also likely to have adverse impacts on housebuilding, at least in the short term. In the longer term, even the most optimistic view suggests that increased problems of housing access will arise in some places.

The commitment to replacement investment represents an important acknowledgement that the Right to Buy has consequences that demand new investment in affordable housing, but there are serious doubts about whether the approach being adopted will work, either in volume terms or in providing the social housing that is needed, where it is needed, and at an appropriate cost. The resort to selling high-value council dwellings to fund the Voluntary Right to Buy raises profound questions about priorities and fairness. Housing association tenants are entitled to much larger incentives to buy than are available to private tenants or first-time buyers. At the same time, high-value council properties will be sold when they became vacant – involving an immediate loss of relets available to households in need. It would be more defensible if government pump-primed replacement building so that it would offset the loss of relets from the outset and avoid the stark choice between selling a vacant property to fund the discount for a well-housed household to buy, or letting a property to a household in severe housing need.

The Voluntary Right to Buy in England also raises issues about the geographical redistribution of spending, and whether replacement dwellings are of the type and size and in the locations that are appropriate. In the longer term, a significant proportion of sold housing association dwellings are also likely to become privately rented. This may affect all parts of the stock, but will probably be more pronounced in certain property types and localities. These lettings may provide choices for households seeking to rent, but costs related to benefit expenditure and issues about the quality of property maintenance and management will arise.

Public housing's long goodbye

The Right to Buy was introduced when public housing (council and new towns) was the major alternative to home ownership. Housing associations had a small share of the market and private renting was in long-term decline and offered predominantly older properties with a mixed reputation in terms of condition and management. But council housing was an ageing tenure, and its reputation and quality had been damaged by the poor design and construction of some estates, and especially of multi-storey flats and maisonettes that had been promoted by government subsidies. These and other parts of the stock were also affected by weaknesses in approaches to management and investment in maintenance and improvement.

At the same time developments in other tenures had affected who became tenants in the public sector, with more affluent households more likely to become homeowners, and a shift towards lower-income and vulnerable groups in social housing. The residualisation of council housing was well established before 1980, but the Right to Buy meant it declined in size, the lack of new housing meant it was predominantly an ageing stock with increasing problems of obsolescence, and that residualisation increased more rapidly. The Right to Buy has changed the property size and types that compose the sector and where it is located. Although the Decent Homes programme and other initiatives made improvements in parts of the stock, the overall story of council housing since 1979 has been one of decline. Transfers of council stock to housing associations that became the preferred vehicle for new rented housing and policies on rents and other issues led a number of commentators to refer to the end of council housing.

While council housing declined steadily across the UK, it remained substantial by international standards. In England, however, Pay to Stay and the sale of high-value council dwellings as well as the continued operation of the Right to Buy can be expected to further speed the decline of council housing. Projections of sales under Right to Buy and sales of vacant high-value stock to fund Voluntary Right to Buy in England suggest an annual loss of over 20,000 council dwellings a year, with no immediate replacement, and no certainty of replacement social housing. If housing associations choose to move away from social rented provision towards other housing being promoted by the government, the shortage of social renting will become more chronic. Councils will have even less capacity to address problems of housing shortage, house condition and homelessness, and be more reliant on a private rented sector where rents are higher, tenancies are insecure and quality and management may be poor. Against this background the need to rebuild the public and social rented sectors is an imperative.

Localism and independence

One of the continuing issues raised by the sale of public and social housing concerns local control and independence. In the years before the Right to Buy local authorities tasked with assessing and meeting local housing needs were regarded as best able to decide whether to sell or not: central government should not make decisions that involved considerations it was not informed about. Issues of local need, the nature of the local market and other issues were best addressed locally, and central government could not be expected to be knowledgeable about them. In the event, the same policy, when imposed by central government, generates very different outcomes in different places and for different households. In more recent years the different decisions taken in Scotland and Wales have been based on judgements about need and strategy. By contrast, in England, outcomes affecting different regions, conurbations or more rural areas have not been shaped by needs or strategies, and reflect a centralised political and administrative approach.

Where councils have retained housing stocks, sometimes following ballots of tenants who have rejected stock transfers, central government appears to regard it as legitimate to require them to sell some high-value stock as it becomes vacant. This immediately prevents councils from reletting these properties – to homeless households or others. Because these are properties with high values, they are likely to be mainly more attractive properties in more attractive locations. The requirement to sell is reminiscent of some aspects of the widely criticised discretionary sales policy adopted in the London Borough of Westminster in the 1980s and 1990s. The policy developed in 2015 appears to take insufficient account of the loss of relets or local consequences or the absence of local capacity to affect decisions that impinge on their housing duties and responsibilities. At this level, the extended Right to Buy raises major questions, and there is need for a complete rethink.

The debate about the independence of housing associations in 2015 raised similar issues. Housing associations considered that, in agreeing the Voluntary Right to Buy, they had kept the government at arm's length, protecting their financial viability and ability to make independent decisions. It is easy to agree with the argument that housing associations' detailed policies should not be dictated by central or local government. The growth of housing associations has been supported by public policies, and this has facilitated an approach in which housing associations have not sought to maximise rental incomes or adopt the lowest cost options in management and approaches to tenants and communities. If a new-found independence, emerging from the debates triggered in 2015 in England, changed this tradition, the value of independence might be questioned. For example, if a significant number of housing associations used their independence to adopt policies that took little or no account of the views of tenants or of local needs or of strategies approved by local authorities, the merits of independence could be open to question. If housing associations, as the dominant providers of social rented housing, used their independence to adopt approaches that were indistinguishable from good private landlords, there would be implications for the costs of Housing Benefits and for a range of local public services. A responsible use of independence would mean working with local and central government, and adopting strategies that take account of local political and community views.

Reference to independence is likely to bring forward questions about whose interests independence promotes, and whether boards adopt policies that are in the interests of tenants or households in housing need. And these questions may need to be addressed where governing bodies consist of professionals who have little contact with tenants or communities, which in turn have little or no direct representation. The perceived escape of housing associations from day-to-day interference by government leaves the potential for them to adopt very different strategies with different consequences for people and places. There is likely to be scrutiny of how housing associations use their independence and their relationship with local authorities and communities.

Cost renting and private renting

The Right to Buy was an exhortation policy to expand home ownership and celebrate its popularity. Because of its design, and the generosity of discounts, it expanded home ownership. In England the reflex reaction to the failure to maintain this increased level of home ownership – and to its decline – has been to introduce more of the same. The extension of Right to Buy to housing associations, and the higher discounts that have been introduced, are likely to achieve another short-term expansion of home ownership. But the evidence suggests that, unless the cash incentives associated with Right to Buy purchase are also available when properties are resold, the level of home ownership will settle at a lower level, and private landlords will become responsible for some of the formerly public sector rented housing. Policies to promote home ownership, from Starter Homes to Help to Buy and to Right to Buy, reintroduce subsidies to homeowners in order to influence household choices. But the evidence is that it is difficult to sustain home ownership at levels above 65%. A substantial proportion of households – more in an increasingly unequal society – are unable to buy without considerable subsidy, and investors are better able to buy properties that come on the market than they are. A nation with more homeowners than this is unlikely, and there is a need to have a housing policy based on more than one tenure.

The debate is not then about the relative merits of home ownership and council housing, but about the relative merits of different forms of renting, and about whether the government should intervene to halt the decline of public and social rented housing and to rebuild its capacity. In this debate there are issues about what is best for the government and for households – in terms of costs, rights, security, appropriateness and quality (design and construction, management and maintenance). At its best, private renting delivers comparable services at higher costs, especially in terms of expenditure on Housing Benefit. At its worst, it falls short in every respect. While the cost rent tradition (council and housing associations) in Britain is flawed, it has always generally performed better than private renting in terms of security, quality, repair and maintenance, and is provided at lower rents. A larger cost rent sector would involve lower Housing Benefit costs and leave more opportunity to use resources to invest in good quality housing. Both council and housing association housing involve high debt costs in the early years and maturation that facilitates pooling of costs with older properties with smaller historic debts, cross-subsidising new investment and enabling both older and newer properties to be let at rents below market levels. Rather than a housing policy resting on private renting and home ownership, with government meeting market costs for lower-income households, it makes sense to build a self sufficient cost rent sector with rents below market levels, alongside home ownership. A strategy to expand cost rented provision is the best way of addressing housing problems after 35 years of the Right to Buy. This does not assume there is no role for private renting, nor does it presume the form of cost renting. It is rent levels, quality and security rather than who owns and manages the properties that are the key considerations.

Discounts and proportionality

The continuing use of the term 'Right to Buy' has tended to obscure the constant changes in details relating to qualifying periods, historic costs and maximum discounts. These changes appear to have been based on hunch rather than evidence of what was not working, and it is unlikely that they made the scheme more transparent or better understood. Where there were problems – for example, the relative unpopularity of flats and the problems emerging after their sale – the response was to increase discounts and the incentive to buy. The levels of discount available to individual tenants – rising to 70% – were extraordinary and difficult to present as fair to households in other tenures and who were not entitled to any equivalent subsidy.

The very high discounts seemed more than reasonable and necessary to encourage purchasers, and they appear disproportionate in view of cuts in other expenditures since 2010. These concerns apply even more so to the extension of Right to Buy in England following the 2015 general election. Under the Voluntary Right to Buy, discounts for housing association tenants are paid for by government by selling essential housing assets. This level of funding seems out of step with other actions in a period of austerity or the incentives introduced under Help to Buy or for Starter Homes or shared ownership. And concerns remain that, under the Right to Buy, high discounts distorted choices and increased the risk of abuse while the wider concerns about the long-term impact of the policy were only partly addressed by the commitment to replacement investment. Such generous discounts encourage some people to buy properties that they do not intend to continue to live in – because housing costs will be lower and short-term capital gains more certain than if they buy elsewhere in the market. In the context of reductions in welfare and Housing Benefit payments, it might be expected that such generous grants to purchasers should be reconsidered.

The large discounts that have been associated with Right to Buy and are retained in England generate many of the issues associated with the policy. They lie at the heart of concerns that the policy encourages abuse and speculation and that it is unfair. Its unfairness is in offering such large incentives when other first-time buyers, including those who are paying higher rents, and are living in less attractive properties or are in greater need, are presented, if at all, with much less generous opportunities. The issues about replacement are also complicated if the levels of discount erode the capital receipt so significantly that the possibility of replacement becomes problematic. The policy choices would be more straightforward and the consequences fairer if the levels of encouragement under the Right to Buy were similar to those for other schemes to facilitate access to home ownership. This implies what can be referred to as a 'proportionate' discount system, one in which different schemes that provide incentives for first-time buyers or for access to home ownership do not necessarily aim to be exactly the same, but are comparable and not regarded as excessive by those who have not accessed them or do not qualify to do so. In 2015, in England incentives for first time buyers under other policies were much less than under the RTB: cash incentives for council tenants to move were between £20,000 and £30,000; equity loans for purchase of new homes were worth up to 20% of the value and were repayable on resale; Social HomeBuy and Right to Acquire were generally between £9,000 and £ 16,000; starter homes could qualify for a 20% discounts. The much more generous incentives under the RTB for households which already have a home appear disproportionate by comparison.

Alternatives to the Right to Buy

Presenting the key policy choice as between retaining the Right to Buy or abolishing it presents a false dichotomy. There are alternatives for any sales policy related to the scope for local decision-making, qualification and exemption, discount levels, differences between existing and new tenants and requirements for reinvestment of capital receipts. In England, there are a variety of alternatives involving 'proportionate' discounts and choices and that take into account the development of the Right to Buy and issues of localism and independence. These moderate the costs associated with the Right to Buy in the short and long term, and are applicable to all landlords in the public and social rented sector:

1. A no sales policy
   - Abolish the Right to Buy.
   - No sales to sitting tenants.
   - The option for landlords to offer and receive funding to finance proportionate cash incentives to tenants to help them to buy elsewhere and to encourage mobility.
2. A voluntary sales policy
   - Abolish the Right to Buy.
   - Local discretion for sales to sitting tenants alongside and involving the same proportionate cash incentives as available to tenants to help them to buy elsewhere rather than buy their current home.
3. A Right to Buy with proportionate incentives
   - The Right to Buy is amended to provide sales to sitting tenants alongside and involving the same proportionate cash incentives as available to tenants to help them to buy elsewhere.

The issue of replacement investment arises in options 2 and 3, but if the volume of sales is moderated by proportionate discounts, this is likely to be a less significant issue than under existing policies in England. In either case, the sale of vacant properties to facilitate other sales should be a matter for local decision-making, and only be possible where other new lettings come on stream to replace the loss of relets. Each of these options requires funding, and this should either be generated within each landlord's business (and not involve transfers between landlords) or be directly from government. Funding the sales of properties is more manageable if proportionate discounts are involved, and this also increases the opportunity to use public funding to develop an effective cost rent system through new investment in social and public housing.

Conclusions

Whatever view is taken of the opportunities the Right to Buy has presented for some households in the past, after 35 years, the challenges of the housing situation in 2016 demand some review of approaches. A definitive and comprehensive evaluation of the consequences of the policy over different timescales and locations in the future would be valuable. In the absence of this there are serious concerns that suggest the need to revise the policy and locate it within a more effective strategy to address housing needs for different groups in different places. This is especially true in England. What is needed goes beyond a policy related to selling public and social rented housing, and beyond a policy to expand home ownership. It is more important to develop a policy that provides good quality secure and affordable public and social housing.

An expanded social rented sector operating alongside a well-functioning home ownership and private rented sector would be a key element in such a policy. It would provide the best use for public expenditure, and the best chance for a planned and sustained investment to address shortages and the need for renewal, while limiting the volatility associated with market providers. In this context there could be a continuing role for sales policies, but the levels of discount or cash incentives should be proportionate, and cash incentives could be used more consistently and fairly to provide choice and stimulate mobility.

These approaches are more in line with concerns about homes for locals that are relevant for all locations and especially articulated in rural areas. They also imply developing a policy approach that enables local communities and councils to exercise influence rather than assuming that distant housing association boards or central government administrations know best.

REFERENCES

Apps, P. (2015) 'Right to Buy to Let', *Inside Housing*, 14 August (www.insidehousing.co.uk/right-to-buy-to-let/7011233.article).

Atkinson, R. and Goodlad, R. (2002) *Reforming house sales in the social rented sector*, Belfast: Northern Ireland Federation of Housing Associations.

Bassett, K. (1980a) 'The sale of council houses as a political issue', *Policy & Politics*, vol 8, no 3, pp 290-307.

Bassett, K. (1980b) 'Council House sales in Bristol: 1960-1979', *Policy & Politics*, vol. 8, no 3, pp 324-333.

Bentley, S., Cloke, M., Murie, A. and Walsh, M. (2014) *From Right to Buy to private rented housing in Birmingham*, Birmingham: Birmingham City Council.

Birrell, D. and Murie, A. (1980) *Government and politics in Northern Ireland,* Dublin: Gill & Macmillan.

Body, W.S. (1928) *Birmingham and its city managers*, Birmingham: Stanford and Mann.

Bowley, M. (1945) *Housing and the state 1919-1944*, London: George Allen & Unwin.

Brown, C. (2015) 'Fact-checking: are housing associations failing to build?', *Inside Housing*, 23 July (www.insidehousing.co.uk/analysis-and-data/fact-checking-are-housing-associations-failing-to-build/7010945.article).

Burrows, R., Ford, J. and Wilcox, S. (2000) *Housing finance review 2000/2001*, York: Joseph Rowntree Foundation.

City of Birmingham (1939) *City of Birmingham handbook*, Birmingham: Birmingham City Council.

Clarke, A., Jones, M., Oxley, M. and Udagawa, C. (2015) *Understanding the likely poverty impacts of the extension of Right to Buy to housing association tenants*, York: Joseph Rowntree Foundation.

Communities Scotland (2002) *Guidance on the modernised Right to Buy*, Edinburgh: Communities Scotland.

Conservative Party (1970) *A better tomorrow*, London: Conservative Party.

Conservative Party (1974a) *Firm action for a fair Britain*, London: Conservative Party.

Conservative Party (1974b) *Putting Britain first*, London: Conservative Party.

Conservative Party (1979) *Conservative Party manifesto*, London: Conservative Party.

Conservative Party (2015) *Conservative Party manifesto, 2015*, London: Conservative Party.

Copley, T. (2014) *From Right to Buy to Buy to Let*, London: Greater London Authority/London Assembly Labour.

Davis, D. and Field, F. (2012) *Right to Buy 2.0*, London: Institute for Public Policy Research.

DCLG (Department for Communities and Local Government) (2006) *Assessment of the impact of the cost of repairs for Right to Buy leaseholders*, London: HMSO (http://webarchive.nationalarchives.gov.uk/20120919132719/http:/www.communities.gov.uk/documents/housing/pdf/153086.pdf).

DCLG (2010) *Local decisions: A fairer future for social housing*, November, London: DCLG.

DCLG (2011) *Laying the foundations: A housing strategy for England*, London: DCLG.

DCLG (2012a) *Statutory Instrument 2012/734*, London: DCLG.

DCLG (2012b) *Reinvigorating the Right to Buy and One for One Replacement, Impact Assessment*, London: DCLG.

DCLG (2013) *Statutory Instrument 2013/677*, London: DCLG.

DCLG (2014) *Statutory Instrument 2014/1915*, London: DCLG.

DCLG (2015) 'Historic agreement will extend Right to Buy to 1.3 million more tenants', 7 October, Prime Minister's Office.

DCLG (live tables), www.gov.uk/government/statistical-data-sets/live-tables-on-house-building. www.gov.uk/government/statistical-data-sets/live-tables-on-social-housing-sales.

DETR (Department of the Environment, Transport and the Regions) (1998a) *Secure tenants' RTB: Proposals to change the maximum discount cash limit on RTB and other home ownership incentive schemes in England: A consultation paper*, July, London: DETR.

DETR (1998b) *The Housing (RTB) (Limits on Discount) Order 1998*, SI 1998/2997, London: The Stationery Office.

DETR (2003) *Statutory Instrument 2003/498*, London: The Stationery Office.

DoE (Department of the Environment) (1972) *Circular 56/72*, 13 June, London: HMSO.

DoE (1974) *Circular 70/74*, 19 April, London: HMSO.

DoE (1977) *Housing policy: A consultative document*, Cmnd 6851, London: HMSO.

Dunn, R., Forrest, R. and Murie, A, (1987)T he Geography of Council House Sales in England - 1979-85, *Urban Studies*, vol 24, pp 47-59.

Forrest, R. and Murie, A. (1983) 'Residualisation and council housing: Aspects of the changing social relations of housing tenure', *Journal of Social Policy*, vol 12, no 4, pp 453-68.

Forrest, R. and Murie, A. (1984a) *Right to Buy? Issues of need, equity and polarization in the sale of council houses*, Bristol: School for Advanced Urban Studies, University of Bristol.

Forrest, R. and Murie, A. (1984b) *Monitoring the Right to Buy*, Bristol: School for Advanced Urban Studies, University of Bristol.

Forrest, R. and Murie, A. (1985) *An unreasonable act? Central-local government conflict and the Housing Act 1980*, SAUS Study 1, Bristol: School for Advanced Urban Studies, University of Bristol.

Forrest, R. and Murie, A. (1988) *Selling the welfare state*, London: Routledge.

Forrest, R. and Murie, A. (1990a) *Selling the welfare state* (2nd edn), London: Routledge.

Forrest, R. and Murie, A. (1990b) *Moving the housing market: Council estates, social change and privatization*, Aldershot: Avebury.

Forrest, R., Murie, A. and Gordon, D. (1995a) *The resale of former council homes*, London, Department of the Environment.

Forrest, R., Murie, A., Hawes, D., Bridge, G. and Smart, G. (1995b) *Leaseholders and service charges in former local authority flats*, London: HMSO.

Foulis, M. (1985) *Council house sales in Scotland*, Edinburgh: Central Research Unit, Scottish Office.

Foulis, M. (1987) 'The effects of sales on the public sector in Scotland', in D. Clapham and J. English (eds) *Public housing: Current trends and future developments*, London: Croom Helm.

FSA (Financial Services Authority) (2009) *Mortgage market review*, London, FSA.

Guardian, The (1979) 'Heseltine announces new housing policy', 23 June.

Harloe, M. (1985) *The people's home: Social rented housing in Europe and America*, Oxford: Blackwell.

Hills, J., Bastagli, F., Cowell, F., Glennerster, H., Karagiannaki, E. and McKnight, A. (2013) *Wealth distribution, accumulation, and policy*, CASE Brief 33, London: Centre for Analysis of Social Exclusion, London School of Economics.

Hilton, J.P. (1927) *Britain's first municipal savings bank*, London: Blackfriars Press.

Holmans, A.E. (1987) *Housing policy in Britain: A history*, London: Croom Helm.

Holmans, A.E. (1993) 'The changing employment circumstances of council tenants', in Department of the Environment, *Housing in England*, London: HMSO.

House of Commons (1965) *Debates*, vol 715, col 39.

House of Commons (1981) *Second report of the Environment Committee, Council House Sales, Vol I Report*, HC 366- 1/1980-1, London: HMSO.

House of Commons (2016a) HC 370, House of Commons, Communities and Local Government Committee, *Housing Associations and the Right to Buy*, Second Report of Session 2015-16

House of Commons (2016b) Committee of Public Accounts, *Extending the Right to Buy to housing association tenants*, Thirty-eighth Report of Session 2015-16 HC 880.

Jones, C. (2003) *Exploitation of the Right to Buy scheme by companies*, London: Office of the Deputy Prime Minister.

Jones, C. and Murie, A. (1999) *Reviewing the Right to Buy*, Birmingham: Centre for Urban and Regional Studies, University of Birmingham.

Jones, C. and Murie, A. (2006) *The Right to Buy: Analysis and evaluation of a housing policy*, Oxford: Blackwell.

Jones, G.W. (1969) *Borough politics*, Basingstoke: Macmillan.

Kemeny, J. (1981) *The myth of home ownership: Public versus private choices in housing tenure*, London: Routledge.

Kerr, M. (1988) *The RTB: A national survey of tenants and buyers of former council houses*, London: HMSO.

Lund, B. (2016) *Housing politics in the United Kingdom: Power, planning and protest*, Bristol: Policy Press.

Lynn, P. (1991) *The Right to Buy: A national follow-up survey of tenants of council homes in England*, London: HMSO.

Malpass, P. (1990) *Reshaping housing policy: Subsidies, rents and residualisation*, London: Routledge.

Malpass, P. (2000) *Housing associations and housing policy: A historical perspective*, Basingstoke: Macmillan.

Malpass, P. and Murie, A, (1987) *Housing policy and practice*, second edition, Macmillan, Basingstoke.

Marsh, A., Kennett, P., Forrest, R. and Murie, A. (2003) *The impact of the 1999 changes to the Right to Buy discount*, London: HMSO, Office of the Deputy Prime Minister.

Merrett, S. (1979) *State housing in Britain*, London: Routledge & Kegan Paul.

MHLG (Ministry of Housing and Local Government) (1952) Circular 64/52, London: MHLG.

MHLG (1960) Circular 5/60, London: MHLG.

MHLG (1967) Circular 24/67 London: MHLG

MHLG (1968) Circular 42/68, London: MHLG.

Morton, A. (2012) *Ending expensive social tenancies*, London: Policy Exchange.

Murie, A. (1975) *The sale of council houses*, Birmingham: Centre for Urban and Regional Studies, University of Birmingham.

Murie, A. (1983) *Housing inequality and deprivation*, London: Heinemann.

Murie, A. (1989) *Lost opportunities? Council house sales and housing policy in Britain 1979-89*, Working Paper 80, Bristol: School for Advanced Urban Studies, University of Bristol.

Murie, A. (2008a) *Moving homes: The Housing Corporation 1964-2008*, London: Politico's.

Murie, A. (2008b) 'Social housing privatisation in England', in K. Scanlon and C. Whitehead (eds) *Social housing in Europe II*, London: London School of Economics, pp 241-60.

Murie, A. (2014) 'Housing and neighbourhoods: What happened after the sale of state housing to sitting tenants in England?', in K. Scanlon, C. Whitehead and M.F. Arrigiotia (eds) *Social housing in Europe*, Chichester: Wiley Blackwell, pp 415-32.

Murie, A. and Leather, P. (2000) *A profile of housing executive sold properties in Northern Ireland*, Birmingham: CURS, University of Birmingham.

Murie, A. and Wang, Y.P. (1992) *The sales of public sector dwellings in Scotland 1979-91*, Edinburgh: School of Planning and Housing, Edinburgh College of Art/Heriot-Watt University.

National Audit Office (2016) Memorandum for the House of Commons Committee of Public Accounts, Department for Communities and local Government, *Extending the Right to Buy*, www.nao.org.uk

NIHE (Northern Ireland Housing Executive) (1992) *House sales review*, Belfast: NIHE Research Unit

NIHE (2001) *The resale of NIHE housing*, Belfast: NIHE Research Unit.

Niner, P. (1976) *Local housing policy and practice*, Birmingham: University of Birmingham.

O'Carroll, A. (1994) 'The development of owner occupation in Edinburgh 1918-1939', PhD Thesis, Heriot-Watt University, Edinburgh.

O'Carroll, A. (1996) 'Historical perspectives on tenure development in urban Scotland', in H. Currie and A. Murie (eds) *Housing in Scotland*, Coventry: Chartered Institute of Housing.

ONS (Office for National Statistics) (2015) 'Economics statistics classifications', 30 October (www.ons.gov.uk/ons/guide-method/classifications/na-classifications/index.html).

Parker, R.A. (1967) *The rents of council houses*, London: Bell.

Parkin, E. (2015) *Comparison of Right to Buy policies in England, Scotland, Wales and Northern Ireland*, House of Commons Briefing Paper No 07174, 19 August.

Pawson, H., Satsangi, M., Jones, C. and Leishman, C. (2002) *Assessing and predicting the long-run impact of the Right to Buy*, Edinburgh: Communities Scotland.

Pawson, H. and Watkins, C. (1998) 'The resale of former public sector homes in rural Scotland', *Scottish Geographical Magazine*, vol 114, no 3, pp 157-63.

Pawson, H., Watkins, C. and Morgan, J. (1997) *Right to Buy resales in Scotland*, Edinburgh: Scottish Office Central Research Unit.

Perry, J., Wilcox, S. and Williams, P. (2015) *Selling off the stock*, London: Chartered Institute of Housing.

Pooley, C.G. (ed) (1992) *Housing strategies in Europe, 1880-1930*, Leicester: Leicester University Press.

Richmond, P. (1979) 'The sale of council houses – A local study in the City of Worcester', BSc Dissertation, Department of Geography, University of Bristol.

Richmond, P. (1980) 'The sale of council houses in Worcester', *Policy & Politics*, vol 8, no 3, pp 316-317.

Rowlands, R. and Murie, A. (2008) *Evaluation of the social HomeBuy pilot scheme for affordable housing*, Final Report, London: Department for Communities and Local Government.

Scottish Development Department (1972) Circular 19/1972, 9 March.

Scottish Development Department (1974) Circular 36/1974, 9 July.

Scottish Executive (2006) *The Right to Buy in Scotland – Pulling together the evidence, A report to Parliament on the effect of the Right to Buy in practice*, Edinburgh: Scottish Executive.

Scottish Government (2013) *Safeguarding Scotland's social housing*, 3 July.

Scottish Government (live tables), www.gov.scot/Topics/Statistics/Browse/Housing-Regeneration/HSfS/SalesSittingTenants. www.gov.scot/Topics/Statistics/Browse/Housing-Regeneration/HSfS/SalesSittingTenants

Shelter (2012) *Department for Communities and Local Government consultation: Reinvigorating the Right to Buy and One for One replacement*, London: Shelter.

Sprigings, N. and Smith, D.H. (2012) 'Unintended consequences: Local Housing Allowance meets the Right to Buy', *People, Place and Policy Online*, vol 6, no 2, pp 58-75.

Sutcliffe, A. and Smith, R. (1974) *A history of Birmingham 1939-70*, Oxford: Oxford University Press.

Turkington, R. and Watson, C. (2015) 'Housing renewal in England', in R. Turkington and C. Watson (eds) *Renewing Europe's housing*, Bristol: Policy Press.

Tutton, P. and Edwards, S. (2007) *Set up to fail: CAB clients' experience of mortgage and secured loan arrears problems*, London: Citizens' Advice Bureau.

Twine, F. and Williams, N. (1991) *Access, choice and the role of public sector sales in the housing market*, Research Report 18, Edinburgh: Scottish Homes.

Twine, F. and Williams, N. (1993) *The resale of public sector houses in rural Scotland*, Edinburgh: Scottish Homes.

van Kempen, R., Dekker, K., Hall, S. and Tosics, I. (eds) (2005) *Restructuring large housing estates in Europe*, Bristol: Policy Press.

Walker, C. (2014) *Freeing Housing Associations*, London: Policy Exchange, www.policyexchange.org.uk

Welsh Government (2015) *Consultation on the future of the Right to Buy and Right to Acquire – A White Paper for social housing*, Cardiff: Welsh Government (http://gov.wales/consultations/housing-and-regeneration/future-of-right-to-buy/?lang=en).

Wilcox, S. (2006) *A financial evaluation of the Right to Buy*, York: University of York.

Wilcox, S. (2011, 2012, various years) *UK housing review*, London and Coventry: Chartered Institute of Housing/Council of Mortgage Lenders.

Wilcox S., Perry, J. and Williams, P. (2015) (eds) *UK Housing Review*, Coventry: Chartered Institute of Housing.

www.york.ac.uk/res/ukhr/ukhr15/compendium.htm

Wilson, W. (2014) *Housing Association tenants: Right to Buy England*, Standard Note: SN/SP/648, House of Commons Library

Wilson, W. and Bate, A. (2015) *Extending the Right to Buy (England)*, Briefing Paper No 07224, 9 June, London: House of Commons Library.

Zeffman, H. (2015) Right-to-Buy Deal backed by only 55% of housing associations, *The Guardian*, 17 October 2015

Index

A

B

F

G

M

R

S